# From
# BENGAL to PUNJAB
## *THE CUISINES OF INDIA*
### *By*
# SMITA CHANDRA

The Crossing Press, Freedom, California 95019

Library of Congress Cataloging—in—Publication Data

Chandra, Smita.
    From Bengal to Punjab  :   the cuisine of India / by Smita Chandra
    pp. 176  cm.
    Includes index.
ISBN 0-89594-510-X (cloth)  --  ISBN 0-89594-509-6 (pbk.)
    1.  Cookery, India.  I.  Title.
TX724.5.14C373  1991
641.5954 -- dc20

                                                                91-25423
                                                                CIP

# Contents

*To my husband, Sanjeev, who appreciates good food, and to my son, Rohan, who is beginning to.*

*I would like to thank my parents and my in-laws for all the support and encouragement they gave me: my parents for the love of cooking they instilled in me and for the wealth of recipes they shared with me; and my in-laws for imbuing in me their love of good food and the art of spicing it right.*

*I would also like to thank my sisters-in-law, Mamta, Arti, and Rachna, and my aunts and grandmother for sharing their recipes with me. A special word of thanks to my good friend Nina Bassuk for helping me write the section on growing herbs at home and for all the help and advice she has given me over the years.*

*This book would never have been possible without my husband, Sanjeev, who tasted every dish I cooked for this book and was always ready with help, advice, and encouragement whenever I needed it.*

# Preface

Food has always held strong associations for me. I remember having long chats with my mother over the breakfast table when I was home on vacation, so long indeed that my father would find us still deep in conversation when he came home for lunch. I remember treating friends to lunch when some good fortune befell me, and I remember the friendly warmth of my in-law's kitchen where the whole family would help to cook the evening meal, exchanging gossip while tasting the food.

Living in a country such as India, where the cuisine of every state is an adventure in taste, it is small wonder that I associate places with food. As a child growing up in India, I was under the firm impression that American cuisine consisted solely of hot dogs and pizza, which to me seemed a wildly exciting diet. On coming to the United States, I discovered that people here hold similar misconceptions about Indian food. "I love curry" was the first thing most people told me after learning that I was from India. To them, all Indian food was curry and any dish could be Indianized simply by adding all-purpose curry powder.

In fact, an Indian cook probably wouldn't know what to do with curry powder. It is considered a strictly Western innovation; it does not exist in Indian cookery and the word *curry* has no real equivalent in any Indian language. However, South Indian cooks do use fragrant leaves called *karipatta* to aromatize their dishes. The literal translation into English is curry leaves, not to be confused with curry powder. Curry powder is probably derived from the Tamil word *kari*, meaning meat cooked in a hot and spicy sauce.

Although no generic curry powder is used in Indian cuisine, each individual dish does call for a mix of several spices known as *masala*, to be ground fresh every day. This masala may consist of varying proportions of onions, ginger, garlic, coriander (fresh and dried), coconut, whole *garam masala* (an aromatic combination of cinnamon, cardamom, cloves, nutmeg, and black pepper), and poppy seeds.

The creativity of the cook lies in the mastery of spices, which lends individuality to age-old recipes. Therein lies the charm of Indian cuisine, for it not only differs from region to region but also from family to family.

Each region has its own distinctive cuisine, with emphasis on different spices. Dishes from the North, for example, are spiced with cumin seeds and garam masala, whereas South Indian dishes are flavored with coconut, mustard seeds, and curry leaves. Dishes from the West are sweet-sour to the taste. Certain religious taboos apply, too. Hindus do not eat beef and Moslems do not eat pork. The majority of Indians are vegetarian, which is reflected in the many ways any single vegetable can be prepared. For example, potatoes can be cooked with cumin seeds and scallions or with peas and tomatoes or in a myriad of other ways. Vegetables are used not only as main and side dishes but are cleverly transformed into dumplings, appetizers, crepes, snacks, soups, chutneys, pickles, breads, and desserts, clearly demonstrating the versatility of this cuisine.

Until recently, cookbooks were not used in the Indian kitchen. One lived in extended families and carried on the tradition of the family through cooking. Girls learned to cook watching their mothers and grandmothers and took a bit of this heritage with them to their husband's family. Recipes were handed down through generations and each family acquired a distinctive style of cooking within the confines of their regional cuisine. In spite of the many Indian restaurants found in every major city of the world, or perhaps because of them, authentic Indian cuisine still remains largely unrecognized. The bill of fare in an average restaurant continues to be sadly stereotyped, giving the impression that Indian food is overspiced, greasy, and too laborious to prepare at home. Yet simply cooked home-style food is delicious, and there is a plethora of cooking styles to choose from, each more delectable than the next. I hope to convey this to you on these pages.

# Introduction

# Your Indian Shelf

This chapter will acquaint you with all the ingredients you need to cook an Indian meal. If you live in a big city or a fair-sized town, you may not have to go very far to shop for Indian ingredients. Many large supermarkets have Asian sections, where the ingredients you need for Indian cookery can be found. Health food stores, specialty food shops, food co-ops, and Asian grocery stores can supply you with the rest. If there is anything you cannot find in stores, you may order it by mail from the Indian grocers listed at the end of this book.

# Spices and Seasonings

In Indian cuisine, spices are used in various forms—ground, whole, roasted, fried, or soaked in vinegar. Each technique draws out a different aroma and flavor from the same spice. Except for a few, spices have to be cooked in order to release their full fragrance and flavor. The object of spicing is to use just the right combination in each dish so that no single spice overpowers the dish, yet each harmonizes with the other to enhance the flavor of the main ingredient. In some dishes, a single spice may be accentuated and the quantity of other spices and herbs kept down to highlight this fact. However, spices are not used just for their flavor; all have some medicinal and digestive properties as well, and a judicious combination of different spices is used in each meal to help the body digest the food and heal itself.

Spices should be bought whole, and ground in small amounts as needed. Whole spices have a longer shelf life than ground ones, meaning that they hold their flavors better. All spices should be stored in airtight containers in a cool, dark place.

## Asafoetida (*hing*)

This dried gum resin from the roots of certain Indian plants has a strong, pungent aroma and hence is used only in tiny amounts, which are added to hot oil or roasted along with cumin seeds. Since asafoetida is available only at Indian and Pakistani grocers and is definitely an acquired taste, I have made its use optional in some recipes. It is brown and available in both lump and ground form. I would suggest that you buy it in lump form and grind small amounts when required by crushing it with a mortar and pestle or between two sheets of paper, since if stored in its ground form, it is not nearly as pungent and loses its aroma quickly. It is considered a digestive aid and is said to relieve flatulence. Hence it is added to dishes that may cause flatulence, such as lentil and bean dishes.

## Cardamom (*elaichi*)

Although cardamom pods can be of the green or the black variety, in this book only the green type have been used, mainly because they are easily available and are also more fragrant than the black ones. They are about 1/4 inch long, with pale green skin and a pleasant aroma. They can be used whole by frying in oil and adding the food to be cooked to them, or their seeds can be ground and sprinkled over the half-cooked or fully cooked dish. The whole cooked pods can also be ground. Cardamom is an important ingredient in making *garam masala* and is also used in flavoring desserts and teas. Green cardamom pods are available at Indian grocery stores. The bleached buff-colored pods often found in supermarkets lack flavor. Avoid buying ground cardamom.

## Cayenne pepper (*lal mirch*)

Made from dried hot red chillies, cayenne pepper is referred to as chilli powder in India. Because it is very hot, I have used very small amounts in most recipes. If you don't want a dish to be hot, you can eliminate the cayenne from the recipe or adjust the amount to your taste.

## Chillies, whole (*sabut mirch*)

Two kinds of chillies are used in this book: fresh green ones and dried red ones. The green ones are small, 3/4 to 1 inch in length, rich in vitamin A and C, and fiery hot to the taste—the smaller, the hotter. You can buy them from Indian or Asian grocers. Buy a big bunch whenever you find the kind you want and freeze some. The process is simple—just snap off their stalks, wipe the chillies with a paper towel, place them in an airtight plastic bag, and place them in the freezer. You don't need to thaw them before using; they are easily sliced when frozen. To store them fresh in the refrigerator, wipe them with a paper towel and keep them in an airtight container lined with paper towels. They should last for a month or longer. Green chillies are available at Indian grocery stores and can be ordered by mail. If you cannot find green chillies, you may substitute cayenne pepper.

Whole red chillies are used in Indian dishes to add their special aroma and flavor to the food. In general, red chillies are hotter than green chillies. They are often fried in hot oil before being added to the dish.

If you find either variety of chilli too hot to eat, just deseed them to get most of their flavor but not all of their heat. For care in handling fresh chillies, see page 00.

## Cinnamon (*dalchini*)

Although cinnamon can be bought ground or in sticks or chips, I would advise buying sticks. They are used whole in meat, vegetable, and rice dishes and are fried in hot oil to draw out their flavor.

They are also ground to use in making *garam masala*.

## Cloves (*laung*)

Available whole or ground, whole cloves are recommended. You can fry, roast, or grind them according to each recipe.

## Coriander seeds (*sookha dhania*)

The dried light brown seeds of the coriander plant are an important spice in Indian cooking and are used both whole and ground. Although the whole seeds are sometimes fried in oil or roasted before being ground and added to the food, raw ground coriander is used in almost every recipe. It is best to buy whole seeds and grind them as needed. If you buy ground coriander, I suggest you buy it in small amounts, since it loses its aroma and becomes tasteless after awhile.

## Cumin seeds (*jeera*)

A commonly used spice in Indian cooking, cumin seeds resemble caraway seeds in appearance. Their flavor is said to stimulate the appetite and aid digestion. Cumin seeds are available in supermarkets and in Asian and Indian grocery stores in both whole and ground form. Both are used in Indian cooking, the whole seeds sometimes also being roasted and ground for use in raitas (yogurt relishes), salads, and chutneys. To roast cumin seeds, put them in a cast iron or nonstick pan. Dry-roast them, without any oil, over low heat until they are fragrant and change color. This will take just a minute or two. Let cool, then coarsely grind them.

## Fennel seeds (*saunf*)

With a sweet, licoricelike flavor, fennel seeds are very similar to anise seeds in flavor, but are slightly larger. They are used in meat and vegetable preparations and in making pickles. They can be used whole—by roasting them in hot oil with other spices and then adding the food to be cooked to them—or ground, or roasted and ground. In an Indian meal, plain fennel seeds or roasted fennel and cardamom seeds are served as after-dinner palate fresheners.

## Fenugreek seeds (*methi*)

Obtained from the dried, ripe fruits of this annual herb, fenugreek seeds, as well as the fresh green leaves of the plant, are used in Indian cooking. The seeds are brownish yellow and have a strong, bitter flavor and a captivating aroma. They are added to hot oil in which the food will be cooked. During cooking they mellow in flavor and infuse the food with their strong fragrance. They are generally used whole; only small quantities of the ground seeds are added to any dish to prevent it from tasting bitter.

## *Garam masala*

There is no English name for this spice mixture—a fragrant blend of cardamom, cinnamon, cloves, black pepper, and cumin. It is an essential ingredient in most North Indian and Mughlai preparations. To preserve the aroma, the mixture is generally added to foods toward the end of cooking. Although *garam masala* is available commercially, I find it quite inferior to that made at home. The ready-made variety lacks authenticity, because the expensive spices, such as cardamom and cloves, are not used in sufficient quantities. They are replaced by less expensive spices, such as coriander and fenugreek, which diminish the mixture's true zesty flavor. The recipe is given on page 00.

## Ginger, ground (*sonth*)

Made by drying and grinding fresh ginger root, ground ginger is commonly available at all supermarkets. It is especially used in Kashmiri and Mughlai preparations.

## Mustard seeds, black (*rai*)

These round dark brown seeds are an important spice in South Indian cooking. The fresh green leaves of the mustard plant are used to make a popular dish in Punjab called *sarson ka saag*. The seeds are generally used whole, although in Bengali cooking they are often soaked in water and made into a thick paste to be added to the dish. You can buy the seeds at Indian grocery stores.

## Nigella, onion seeds (*kalonji*)

Although these seeds look like onion seeds and smell like onions, they have nothing else in common with the onion plant. They are black and shaped rather like a teardrop, with an oniony, oregano-like aroma. The spice is generally used whole and unroasted; it is important in pickling and is also used in chutneys and meat and vegetable dishes. It is available at Indian and Pakistani grocery stores.

## Nutmeg (*jaiphal*)

Although not used widely in Indian cooking, nutmeg is an important ingredient in *garam masala*. It has a mild, sweet flavor and a gentle aroma. Buy whole nutmeg and grate as required.

## Poppy seeds, white (*khus khus*)

These seeds are quite different from the black poppy seeds commonly sprinkled on breads and rolls. These are cream colored, round, and tasteless in their raw form. They are soaked in water or fried in hot oil with other spices, and then ground to a paste. The paste is added to meat, chicken, and vegetable dishes to add body to the sauce and a mild nuttiness to the flavor.

## Saffron (*kesar*)

These strands are the dried stigma of certain crocuses. Saffron is an expensive spice used sparingly in festive dishes such as *biryanis* (spiced rice), meats, and desserts. It imparts a delicate orange-yellow color to the dish. It is available in thread or ground form in Indian, Pakistani, and Middle Eastern grocery stores.

## Salt, black (*kala namak*)

This salt is available in lump and ground form. In the lump form it is brownish black, which changes to pinkish brown when ground. If you decide to buy it in lump form, you can grind it when required by crushing it with a mortar and pestle. Buying it in ground form is simpler though, and it retains its flavor longer than other ground spices. It has a very distinctive flavor and aroma, goes well with ground roasted cumin seeds, and is an important spice in raitas, salads, and fresh chutneys. It is available in Indian grocery stores; when asking for it, use the Indian name, *kala namak*, to facilitate matters.

## Sesame seeds, white (*safed til*)

These cream-colored seeds have a delicious nutty flavor, especially when roasted or fried. They are sometimes ground and used as a thickener in dishes or fried whole and cooked along with the food.

## Tamarind (*imli*)

Extremely sour and chocolate brown in color, it comes from the tamarind pod. Tamarind is available in paste form, which is easy to use—just dissolve it in warm water. I sometimes add it directly to the food and let it melt while the food cooks.

If using tamarind pulp, soak it in hot water for 30 minutes, squeeze out all the juice, strain, and discard the fibrous residue. Tamarind is used in meat, poultry, and *dal* dishes and in chutneys. It is available at Indian grocery stores.

## Turmeric (*haldi*)

This spice is used extensively all over India as a coloring and flavoring agent, and is also said to have digestive and antiseptic properties. It is commonly available in ground form in most supermarkets.

# Herbs

Sometimes used as a garnish, sometimes pureed for sauces or chutneys, and sometimes cooked along with the food, herbs add their aroma and distinctive flavor to a dish. Herbs such as coriander, curry leaves, fenugreek, and mint are used extensively in Indian cooking to season and aromatize the food. Many herbs used in Indian cookery are now available at large supermarkets, and most of them can be bought at Asian or Indian grocery stores; others, such as fenugreek, are not readily available commercially but can be grown at home. Suggestions on how to grow Indian herbs are given at the end of this chapter.

Because fresh herbs are not always available, dried herbs can be substituted, but lack the fragrance and flavor of the fresh ones. Curry leaves and fenugreek leaves are exceptions; when dried, they retain their fragrance and flavor.

## Coriander (*hara dhania*)

Fresh green coriander leaves, sometimes referred to as cilantro or Chinese parsley, can be bought at well-stocked supermarkets, and Asian, Indian, or Mexican grocery stores. The leaves are used as a garnish, although the upper, less fibrous stems are sometimes added to the leaves when pureeing them for sauces or chutneys.

To store fresh coriander for up to several weeks, immerse its roots in a jar of water, cover the jar loosely with a plastic bag, and refrigerate. If you have bought coriander without its roots, line an airtight container with paper towels and put the unwashed leafy coriander stems in it. Cover and refrigerate. It is also possible to pat dry the leafy stems with a paper towel and freeze them in an airtight plastic bag, but I do not find them as flavorful.

## Curry leaves (*karipatta*)

These fragrant green leaves are an essential part of South Indian cooking. They are added to hot oil along with mustard seeds to flavor the food that is then cooked. Curry leaves can also be ground for use in chutneys, or roasted in barbecued foods. Fresh curry leaves are available at some Indian grocery stores and can be ordered by mail. Stored in a plastic bag in the refrigerator, they should keep for 10 to 12 days. If you cannot find fresh leaves, you may substitute dried ones. In this book I have called for the dried variety, since they are easily available at Indian grocery stores.

## Fenugreek leaves (*methi*)

Fenugreek leaves are very aromatic and taste mildly bitter; a lot of lemon juice is used in fenugreek dishes to counteract the bitterness. The fenugreek stalks are never used—they are too bitter and fibrous. Some Indian grocery stores stock fenugreek leaves but the plant can easily be grown at home. The dried leaves are readily available at Indian or Pakistani grocery stores. In this book, do not substitute dried leaves for fresh ones or vice versa unless specifically mentioned in the recipe.

## Mint leaves (*podhina*)

Although there are many varieties of mint, the type used in India and in this book is peppermint. Also known as garden mint, it has dark green leaves and a distinctive flavor and aroma. Mint goes especially well with meat and the two are often used together in Mughlai preparations, tandoori dishes, *biryanis* (spiced rice), and chutneys. Mint leaves can be stored in a plastic bag in the refrigerator for a week.

# Your Indian Herb Garden

Even though some herbs used in Indian cookery, such as coriander and mint, are available at large supermarkets, other herbs are found only in Indian grocery stores or specialty food stores. Sometimes when you need the herb right away, it is difficult to make a trip to the store. It's much simpler to walk to your garden or herb window box and snip a few sprigs.

Herbs are hardy and easy to grow. All they need is good potting soil, adequate water, and sunlight. They can grow in the backyard, between rows of other plants, or in flower pots or window boxes. Here are some suggestions on how to plant Indian herbs. Instructions for growing green chillies are also included.

## Coriander

Buy whole seeds you would use for cooking. Soak them in cold water for at least 3 to 4 hours or overnight. Choose a sunny spot and see that the soil has no stones or weeds and has been freshly turned over. Plant the seeds in a row approximately 1/8 inch beneath the surface, or scatter them evenly over the area to be planted and cover them with a 1/8-inch layer of potting soil. Water the area once daily until the plants appear, then water on alternate days. The shoots will be ready to pick in 6 to 8 weeks. They will keep growing back as you snip off the top portions, so do not uproot them. Once the flowers and the seeds appear on the plant, the leaves start losing their fragrance and the stalks become too woody, so it is advisable to use up the plant before then.

If you are planting in a flower pot or window box, make sure that the container is at least 6 inches deep and has a hole at the bottom for drainage. Keep it in a sunny spot. You can grow coriander indoors all year long.

Coriander plants can withstand a fair amount of cold. You can plant them outdoors from mid-April to early October. Leave the roots of the last crop in the soil; they will grow back in spring.

### Mint

The variety of mint used in Indian cookery is peppermint, also called garden mint. It is often found growing wild in lawns and gardens. Many people regard it as a tiresome weed, since it spreads with abandon. If you do not have any in your garden, plant a cutting 2 to 3 inches deep and keep it moist and cool until it begins growing. You will soon have some to share.

### Fenugreek

Follow the directions for growing coriander. When picking shoots for cooking, you will have to uproot the plant, since, unlike coriander, it does not grow back. Once the flowers and pods appear, it becomes less fragrant; use up the plant before then. The shoots should be about 6 inches tall for the leaves to mature and become mellow tasting. Leaves of younger plants can be quite bitter. Fenugreek can be grown from mid-April to early October.

### Green chillies

These plants can be grown successfully indoors in flower pots or outdoors. To obtain seeds, slit open a fresh green chilli and shake out the seeds onto a plate. Let them dry at room temperature overnight. Start them indoors in early April; if they will be grown outside, transplant them when they are established to a very sunny spot in the garden. The chillies will take 10 to 12 weeks to appear. Once the frost comes you can pot the plants and keep them in a sunny spot indoors.

# Essences (*ruh*)

Basically extracts from different flowers, essences are used to perfume foods such as *biryanis* (spiced rice), desserts, and cool drinks. The two most commonly used varieties are *kewra* essence and rose essence.

Kewra essence is also known as screw pine essence and is an extract of the flower's petals. It has a strong aroma that goes well with sweet foods, such as desserts, and drinks. Just a drop or two is enough to perfume the food. It can be bought at Indian and Pakistani grocery stores labeled as kewra water or kewra essence. If you cannot find it, you may use rose essence in its place or omit it entirely (although the dish will lose some of its authenticity).

Rose essence is extracted from small fragrant red roses. Its strong aroma brings a breath of the garden into the desserts and cool drinks. It is available in Indian and Pakistani grocery stores. In its place you can use rose water, which is diluted rose essence.

# Rice

This is the staple food of two thirds of India's population. Not surprisingly, each region has created a myriad of rice dishes, each varying in flavor and texture. Rice is ground and used to make crepes, dumplings, savories, and sweets; it is cooked with meat and vegetables to form *pullaos* and *biryanis* (spiced rice); and it is cooked plain to be used as a complement to the spicy curries and dals that accompany it.

There are two varieties of rice commonly used in Indian cooking—long grain and basmati. Long-grain rice is used for everyday meals. The grains, when cooked, are light, fluffy, and do not stick together.

Basmati rice, a variety of long-grain rice, is reserved for special occasions, since it is more expensive. The most popular variety is Dehradun basmati rice from Dehradun in the state of Uttar Pradesh. Basmati rice has an exquisite aroma and delicate, long, slim grains; it is tender, though not mushy, to the touch. Even plain basmati rice is a delight. When made into pullaos or *biryanis* (spiced rice), it is a gastronomical treat.

Although basmati rice costs a little more than regular long-grain rice, it is worth buying because it transforms a dish from ordinary to superb. Precleaned basmati rice is available at Indian grocery stores in bags of 2 to 11 pounds. Supermarkets stock it but at a much higher price.

# Legumes

Dried legumes include lentils (also known as *dals* in India), split peas, dried beans, and chick-peas. Their uses are innumerable. They are cooked to a puree and flavored with spiced butter or ghee; they are soaked in water, ground to a paste, and formed into dumplings, crepes, or breads; and they are cooked with meat, rice, or vegetables to form hearty stews. Each kind of legume has a different flavor, texture, and color; all are important sources of protein. Stored in airtight containers in a cool, dry place, they have an indefinite shelf life. Dried legumes should be picked over, washed well, and soaked in water before cooking. The legumes used in this book are described below. When ordering them from Indian grocery stores, use their Indian names, since not all grocers are familiar with the English translations.

## Black gram bean, split and hulled (*dhuli urad dal*)

Sold split and hulled, this legume is cream-colored and has a viscous texture when cooked.

## Black gram bean, whole (*sabut urad*)

Sold whole and unhulled, this legume has a blackish gray skin and a slightly glutinous texture when cooked.

## Lentil, whole brown (*sabut masoor dal*)

Also known as Egyptian lentils, this dal is saucer-shaped and brown and is used whole and unhulled. It is commonly available in supermarkets.

## Lentil, yellow (*arhar* or *tur dal*)

Golden yellow in color, this dal, sold hulled and split, is the most commonly used variety.

## Mung bean, split (*dhuli moong dal*)

Sold split and hulled, this legume is pale yellow, has a delicate flavor, and is easy to digest.

## Mung bean, whole (*sabut moong*)

Also called green gram bean, this pale green and slightly cylindrical legume is commonly used for sprouting in Chinese cuisine. It is sold in supermarkets as well as Asian and Indian grocery stores.

## Split pea, yellow (*chana dal*)

This pale yellow legume is the Indian version of the familiar yellow split pea. Chana dal is slightly smaller in size, and when cooked imparts a meaty flavor to a dish. In Indian cuisine, it is cooked alone or with vegetables or meat. Chana dal is sold in Indian grocery stores in both raw and roasted form. The raw type is best. You may also substitute the supermarket yellow split pea.

### Other peas and beans

Chickpeas (or garbanzo beans), red kidney beans, and black-eyed peas are available in supermarkets in dried or canned form. You may use either canned or frozen beans, or soak dry ones overnight and cook them in enough water to cover until tender. Drain them before using. In the recipes in this book calling for peas, use green peas (either frozen or cooked fresh) unless otherwise specified.

# Other Ingredients

### Chapati flour (*atta*)

Available only in Indian grocery stores, chapati flour is very finely ground whole wheat flour used in making most Indian breads, such as *chapatis*, *parathas*, and *puris*. If you cannot find chapati flour, use the substitutes suggested in the recipes.

### Chickpea flour (*besan*)

Made by grinding dried chickpeas to a powder, this flour is used to make *pakora* (dumpling) batter, crepes, and sweetmeats, and is also used as a thickener for sauces. It is pale yellow and extremely nutritious. You can buy it from Indian grocery stores, where it is also called gram flour, or from specialty or health food stores. Store it in an airtight container in a cool, dry place.

### Coconut (*nariyal*)

Used extensively in Indian cooking, coconuts are an ingredient in sweetmeats, sauces, and stir-fries. Coconut milk is used in poultry or meat dishes. Coconuts are readily available in supermarkets. Look for the ones with no cracks or mold on the surface; shake them and listen for the slosh of coconut water inside. Store them in the refrigerator. Grated coconut can be frozen in an airtight plastic bag.

### Coconut flakes and powder

Unsweetened dried coconut flakes, available in well-stocked supermarkets and specialty food stores, are used to make chutneys and sauces. Unsweetened desiccated coconut powder is available at Indian grocery stores and is an excellent thickening and flavoring agent for sauces.

### Fenugreek leaves, dried (*sookhi methi*)

Also referred to as *kasoori methi*, these highly aromatic leaves of the fenugreek plant come from Qasur in Pakistan, which produces the best fenugreek. The leaves are available at Indian and Pakistani grocery stores.

### Ginger root, fresh (*adrak*)

This root with its knobby shape and brown skin is used in almost all Indian recipes. It has a sharp, pungent flavor and is said to have digestive properties. Although it is usually peeled before being finely chopped, minced, or grated, I prefer to use it unpeeled—for the fiber it adds to my diet; the difference in flavor is marginal. When buying fresh ginger root, look for pieces that have a taut skin. Break a piece open to make sure the inside flesh is not too fibrous.

### Mango, green cooking (*hare aam*)

Available in the summer months at Indian grocery stores, unripe green mangoes are used for pickles, chutneys, sherbets (cool drinks), and general cooking purposes. They are sour and impart a distinctive flavor to the foods. They can be ordered by mail from Indian grocery stores.

### Mango pulp

Available canned at Indian grocery stores, mango pulp is excellent in cool drinks, ice creams, and desserts. Once the can is opened, store the pulp in an airtight container in the refrigerator, but use it quickly, since even with refrigeration it does not last very long.

# Kitchen Tools and Appliances

You do not need to restock your kitchen to cook authentic Indian meals. If you have a few basic utensils, such as heavy-bottomed pans, a rolling pin, slotted spoons, graters, mixing bowls, tongs, and sharp knives, you can begin. There are, however, a few tools and appliances which, while not essential, do make life easier in the kitchen.

## Deep-fat fryer, *karhai*, or wok

The karhai is ideal for frying *pakoras*, *koftas*, and *puris* because it allows you to use relatively small quantities of oil and still be able to submerge the food completely. It is very similar to a Chinese wok, so you can substitute one for the other. If you do not have a wok, you can use a deep-fat fryer.

## Electric coffee grinder

Although many spices can be bought already ground, the best results come from buying whole spices and grinding them just before using, since ground spices lose freshness and flavor if kept for long periods. A blender or food processor cannot grind whole spices finely enough. A coffee grinder is ideally suited to grind small amounts of whole spices. Lacking that, a mortar and pestle or a spice mill can be used.

## Food processor or blender

I would suggest owning both if possible. The food processor saves the day when you must grate, mince, or slice large amounts of food (for parties), whereas the blender works best for finely grinding ingredients for chutneys and herbed sauces, and for mixing coconut and water to make coconut milk. If you do not have a food processor, however, a good knife and a hand grater work fine.

## Griddle

Because many Indian breads are cooked on top of the stove instead of in the oven, a griddle is neces- sary. I find the nonstick variety best for shallow-fried breads, such as parathas, and for making chapatis too. A large cast-iron pan or any large frying pan is a good substitute.

## Large nonstick pan with a lid

Nonstick pans are useful to have in the kitchen because they allow you to use less cooking oil. It is also easy to brown meats and cook thick sauces without burning or scorching them.

## Skewers

Metal or bamboo skewers are necessary for barbecuing foods. If you use bamboo skewers, immerse them in cold water an hour beforehand to prevent them from burning and disintegrating.

# Basic Techniques

Indian cooking employs a number of techniques designed to bring out the best possible flavor of each ingredient used in the dish. At first sight some may seem a little unfamiliar, but after reading through this section and trying out these techniques a few times, you will find them quite easy to master.

## Thickening

If you have cooked Indian food before, you will have noticed that flour is not used as a thickener for sauces. A lighter, more flavorful sauce with a richer color results from using onions, ginger, garlic, and yogurt or tomatoes. Yogurt is usually added after the onions, ginger, and garlic have been sauteed. It imparts a creamy texture and a subtle tartness. Because yogurt tends to curdle at high temperatures, care must be taken to incorporate it properly into the sauce. The first step is to beat it lightly with a spoon for a few seconds until it becomes smooth.

Then reduce the heat to low and add the yogurt to the pan by the spoonful, stirring and blending each batch into the sauce before adding the next. Once all the yogurt has been added, the dish should be cooked for 2 to 3 minutes or more to eliminate the raw flavor.

## Marinating

This is an essential step in barbecuing food. Some stovetop cooking also requires meat or poultry to be marinated. This helps tenderize the meat and allows the flavors of the marinade to permeate it. The marinade can have as its base yogurt; spices and herbs; onion, tomato, nuts, and spices; or any combination of the above. In barbecued foods, the marinade is also used for basting to keep the meat or vegetable from drying out.

## Handling chillies

Three kinds of chillies are used in Indian cuisine: the fresh hot green variety, the dried whole red ones, and ground red chillies (cayenne pepper). All should be handled with extreme care; avoid touching your face and eyes until you have washed your hands with soap, and keep chillies out of the reach of children, since the juice can burn the eyes. If you find the whole green or red chillies too hot to eat, deseed them by slitting open one side or slicing off the stalk and removing the seeds. Most of the recipes in this book call for 1/4 teaspoon cayenne pepper. You can omit it entirely if you wish, or adjust it to your taste.

## Refrigerating and freezing

Indian food can be cooked a few hours up to a day or two in advance and refrigerated. In fact, cooking meat, poultry and chickpea dishes a little ahead of time actually enhances their flavor by giving the food time to absorb the aroma of the spices. Leftover meat, poultry, and vegetable dishes can also be successfully frozen. Rice dishes, yogurt raitas, salads, and chutneys cannot be frozen with good results.

If you do not have the time to cook elaborate meals, you can double most recipes and freeze half for later use. You can also make the sauce for the dish (such as a sauteed onion, tomato, ginger, and garlic sauce) and keep it frozen until needed. Food can remain frozen for up to a month. If you notice that the aroma and flavor of the spices and herbs have dimmed somewhat from being in the freezer, add 1/2 teaspoon *garam masala* or some chopped fresh coriander or mint to the dish to revive it. These should be mixed in after warming the food and before serving it. Always thaw food overnight in the refrigerator and warm it in a low oven (200°F), or in a microwave oven set on high heat, to keep the texture of the food intact and to allow the food to reabsorb the juices and flavors of the sauce.

## Cooking with herbs

Fresh herbs add a delightful fragrance to sauces and heighten their flavor. Chopped coriander leaves are often used as a garnish, or mixed into the food just before serving. Mint goes well with meat—it is used in barbecued dishes and *biryanis* (spiced rice).

## Tempering (*baghar*)

In this technique, oil, ghee, or butter is heated and spices such as asafoetida and cumin, or mustard seeds and curry leaves, or other whole spices are added to it. Chopped ginger, garlic, and chillies can also be added. When the spices brown or puff up, the seasoned oil is poured over the cooked dish, or uncooked food is added to the seasoned oil, covered, and allowed to cook. Some form of tempering is used in all recipes, usually at the start of the cooking. This technique is especially important in making dals, although in this case tempering is used just before serving to heighten the aroma of the spices. Since different spices have different burning temperatures, when adding them to the oil always follow the sequence listed in the recipe.

## Dry-roasting spices (*sookha masala bhoonana*)

Many of the recipes in this book call for dry-roasting spices together. This is done by heating a heavy-bottomed (preferably cast-iron) pan over low heat and adding whole spices or nuts. No oil or butter is used, and the pan is shaken a few times to ensure that the spices roast evenly. In just a few minutes, the spices turn a shade or two darker in color and start smelling fragrant. They are then allowed to cool and are ground. In foods that are not going to be cooked, such as raitas (yogurt relishes) and salads, dry-roasting the spices is essential. In some recipes, a combination of fried and roasted spices is used.

## Deep-frying (*talna*)

Many Indian foods, especially appetizers, are deep-fried. In Indian homes, frying is done in a karhai, which is similar to a Chinese wok. Vegetable oil is generally used as a frying medium. For the best results, dry the food with a paper towel before frying it or before dipping it in batter (if used). Moisture inhibits proper frying and causes the oil to splutter dangerously. Batter, which is sometimes used to coat food before deep-frying, helps seal in the juices and at the same time keeps the food from absorbing too much oil. It also forms a crisp crust on the food.

To deep-fry, heat about 1 cup vegetable oil in a karhai or wok over medium-high heat. When you see a thin shimmer of vapor rising from the oil, test whether it is hot enough for cooking by dropping a small portion of the batter or food into it. It should rise to the surface within seconds. Adjust the heat to the requirements of the recipe and gently drop in the pieces of food to be deep-fried. Add only as many as the pan can hold in a single layer, since overcrowding will cause the food to cook unevenly. The food should be almost totally immersed in the oil. Once the underside has been cooked, use a slotted spoon or spatula to gently turn it over. It should be evenly golden brown on all sides when finished. Lift it out of the oil with a slotted spoon and drain it on a paper towel that has been placed on a plate. Oil left in the pan at the end of cooking should be discarded, since it can turn rancid and spoil the food that is cooked in it.

## Braising (*korma*)

This technique involves cooking food slowly over low heat in a heavy-bottomed pan with a tight-fitting lid. It is used for most of the meats and vegetables in this book. The food is cooked in a combination of yogurt, cream, tomato puree, and water, with all or some of these ingredients used in any given recipe. Because very little cooking liquid is used, the finished food has a thick sauce clinging to it. Braising can be done in several different ways. The meat can be cooked directly in the marinade; it can be taken out of the marinade, browned lightly in oil, and then braised in the marinade; or it can be braised in the oven with the dish tightly covered with aluminum foil. Spicing braised foods is done in stages to achieve the perfect blend of flavors. Some of the spices may first be fried in oil, then ground and mixed into the marinade, or raw ground spices may be mixed into the marinade and the spiced marinade poured into the hot spiced oil. The final batch of spices, usually the *garam masala*, is added toward the end of cooking to preserve the aroma.

## Browning onions, ginger, and garlic (*pyaz ka masala bhoonana*)

This technique should be mastered fairly early, since almost all the recipes in this book call for it to some degree. Although not difficult, browning does require a certain amount of patience. You have to be around to stir the onions frequently to ensure even browning. It is best not to rush this process; I have given the approximate time it will take for each recipe. When frying onions, I like to start out over medium heat and then reduce the heat if needed.

Opinions are divided about when to add ginger and garlic to the recipe. Some people like to chop them finely and add them to the onions after they have browned; others, including me, prefer to fry them lightly in oil before adding the onions. I find that grating or mincing the ginger and garlic, instead of chopping them, improves the texture of the sauce.

## Barbecuing

In India, kebabs, *tikkas*, and tandoori preparations are cooked in a tandoor, a huge clay pit sunk into the ground with a small mouth through which skewered food is lowered onto the glowing charcoals. The clay imparts to the food a wonderful earthy aroma, which is characteristic of tandoori cuisine. Except for this aroma, which only a tandoor can impart, I find that most tandoori dishes can be cooked on a standard charcoal grill. Regularly basting the food with the marinade during grilling prevents the food from drying out and also keeps the flavors and aromas fresh.

The food to be cooked is lifted out of the marinade and placed on the grill. If the food is skewered first, the skewers are laid flat across the grill. Keep the grill 6 to 8 inches away from the coals so that the heat does not sear or burn the food. The food should be cooked over medium heat until tender. Baste it regularly with the marinade and don't allow it to char. Turn it occasionally to ensure even cooking. When the food is done to the desired brownness and tenderness, remove it from the heat and serve it with a sprinkle of lemon juice.

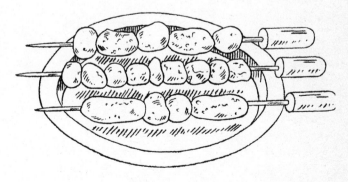

# BASIC RECIPES

Many Indian dishes require one of the following basic ingredients in their preparation.

## Clarified Butter

### *Ghee*

Many Indian cookbooks specify clarified butter, or ghee. Although many families used ghee some years ago, inflated prices and health consciousness have put an end to that. Ghee now is used by the spoonful at the end of cooking to add its wonderful aroma and nutty flavor to the food. In our family, dals are served with spiced ghee poured over them. Eating them any other way is unthinkable.

If you cannot find ready-made ghee (many Asian grocery stores carry it), you may substitute butter or choose to make ghee at home. The technique is very simple. In a heavy-bottomed pan, melt 2 sticks (8 ounces) unsalted butter over low heat. Then increase the heat and let the butter come to a boil. As soon as it starts foaming, stir it once, reduce the heat to very low, and let it simmer for 30 minutes. You will find that particles of residue have settled to the bottom. Let the ghee cool a little, then strain it into a clean container through several layers of cheesecloth, which removes all the particles. Keep the ghee covered in a cool place. There is no need for refrigeration, since it has an indefinite shelf life.

## Coconut Milk

### *Nariyal Ka Doodh*

Cooks in India have to make coconut milk the hard way—break open the coconut, grind the meat, and squeeze out the milk. Canned coconut milk is available in the United States. It tastes almost the same as the homemade variety and using it saves a lot of time; most large grocery stores stock it, and you are certain to find it in Asian grocery stores. If you wish to make it at home, however, here is the procedure.

**Half a fresh coconut**
**7 tablespoons plus 1 cup warm water, or as needed**

Remove the meat from the coconut, place it in the container of a blender with the 7 tablespoons warm water, and grind finely. Line a fine sieve with 2 layers of cheesecloth and strain the coconut pulp, collecting the milk in a bowl placed underneath. Using your hands, squeeze out all the liquid. Place the squeezed-out coconut in a bowl and add the 1 cup warm water. Let it stand for 5 minutes, then repeat the process. If you do not have the amount of milk called for in the recipe, add another 1/2 cup warm water to the coconut residue and extract a third batch of milk, or grate more coconut for richer milk.

Yield: 1 1/4 cups to 1 3/4 cups.

# Cottage Cheese
## *Paneer*

Because the majority of Indians are vegetarian, cottage cheese is used quite a lot to increase the nutritive value of the food. In India it is sold fresh in chunks, rather like tofu; its consistency makes it able to withstand high cooking temperatures without melting. Since the cottage cheese sold in American grocery stores is uncompressed and tends to melt at high temperatures, I have included a recipe for making Indian cottage cheese, which is a simple procedure. When regular cottage cheese can be used in a recipe, I have indicated it.

I find that freezing freshly made cheese for about 1 hour before deep-frying keeps it from crumbling. If you are using frozen cottage cheese, thaw it only partially so it keeps its shape. If the recipe calls for crumbled cottage cheese, you may crumble it directly instead of compressing it.

**1 quart half-and-half *or* 2 quarts milk**
**2 to 3 tablespoons lemon juice**

Bring the half-and-half or milk to a boil in a large heavy-bottomed pan. Add the lemon juice and stir until the curds rise to the top and a clear liquid remains. Turn off the heat and let the pan stand for 5 minutes. Line a fine sieve with 3 layers of cheesecloth and pour the curdled milk through it. Save the whey for use in soups, sauces, rice, or dough-making. Gather up the ends of the cheesecloth to form a pouch and tie it on the faucet over the kitchen sink. Twist the cloth lightly and squeeze out the excess liquid from the cheese with your hands. Let the pouch hang there for 30 minutes, then transfer it to a cutting board and shape it into a patty approximately 4 inches wide and 1/2 inch thick. Fill a large pot with water and place it over

the pouch to compress it. Leave it for about 2 hours. It is now ready to use, or you can remove the cheese from the cheesecloth, cover it with plastic wrap, and freeze it (it will last for up to a month).

Yield: About 1 1/4 cups crumbled cottage cheese *or* 4-inch by 1/2-inch-thick compressed patty.

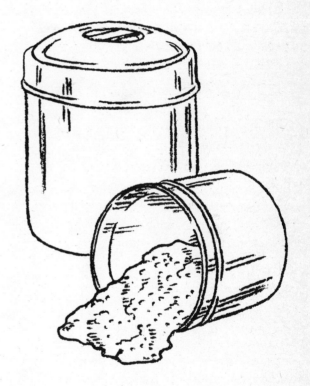

# Garam Masala

Every household in India has its own special blend of *garam masala*, made with the recipe perfected by the family through the generations. Ready-made *garam masala* is available in stores but is considered inferior. The recipe given here belongs to my father-in-law, who is a connoisseur of *garam masala* and uses it liberally in his cooking. You can make this spice blend in batches big enough to last 3 to 4 months. Store it in an airtight container away from heat and light. When I make this *masala*, I don't bother to peel the cardamom pods but grind them skin and all with the rest of the spices. This saves effort, adds fiber to the diet, and doesn't significantly alter the flavor of the *masala*. However, you may want to peel them before grinding.

**1 small nutmeg**
**1 1/2 tablespoons green cardamom pods**
**4 sticks (1 inch each) cinnamon**
**1 tablespoon whole cloves**
**1 teaspoon peppercorns**
**1 teaspoon cumin seeds**

Crush the nutmeg coarsely with a mortar and pestle. Transfer to the container of a clean coffee grinder, add the remaining ingredients, and grind finely. Store in an airtight container.

Yield: About 4 tablespoons.

# Tomato Puree

Homemade tomato puree adds a delightful freshness to certain dishes. The procedure is simple. Allow 3 or 4 medium juicy tomatoes for about 1 cup of puree. Wash the tomatoes, core them, chop coarsely, and whirl to a puree in a blender or food processor. Use as directed in the recipes in this book specifying fresh tomato puree.

Menu
Suggestions

An Indian meal has no distinct courses. All the food is placed on the table at the same time and the diners help themselves to the dishes of their choice. Broad-rimmed steel plates called *thalis* are provided to keep the different sauces from mixing; small steel bowls known as *katoris* hold the more liquid dishes. This authentic tradition is easily adapted to the Western-style meal of distinct courses by serving the appetizers and chutney with the drinks. If you are serving soup, that can be the first course, followed by the main course of the meat or vegetable served with rice or bread.

Traditional family meals have three components: a main dish, which may be meat, poultry, *dal*, or a vegetable; a side dish consisting of a vegetable; and a staple, such as rice or bread. Accompaniments such as pappadams, pickles, chutneys, raitas, and salads are also served.

Using these basic guidelines, you can create your own menus. Meat or poultry can be accompanied by a vegetable. For an all-vegetarian meal, serve the vegetable dish with a dal (a legume, such as lentils, split peas, chickpeas, or dried beans). Your choice of the staple will depend on the dishes served. Dry preparations are easy to scoop up with pieces of bread, whereas soupy ones can be mixed with rice. Food textures can be balanced by combining soupy with dry dishes and soft with crunchy ones. Flavors are enhanced by the judicious use of accompaniments, such as cooling raitas and salads and zesty chutneys and pickles.

To give you an idea of what food goes best with what, this chapter has been laid out in the form of menus. You will find recipes from all over India as well as a number of original recipes, many of them incorporating ingredients readily available in the United States, such as ricotta cheese and puff pastry. Many Indian dishes can be integrated easily into Western meals, either as appetizers or as side dishes. Some dishes are meals in themselves and need only crusty French bread and a salad as accompaniments.

Because beef is not eaten by Hindus in India, there are no beef recipes in this book. However, you can substitute beef in recipes calling for lamb, and adjust cooking times if necessary.

Note: Every recipe in this book, unless otherwise mentioned, serves 4 people. You can easily double or halve it to your own requirements.

---

Zucchini with Onions
*Pyaz Lauki*

Spicy Lentils
*Masoor Masala*

Tomato Salad
*Tamatar Ka Salat*

Turnip Pickle
*Shalgam Ka Achaar*

Long-Grain Rice
*Saaday Chaval*

---

Shrimp with Fenugreek
*Masala Jhinga Methiwala*

Lentils with Cinnamon and Mixed Vegetables
*Masoor Dal Sabziwali*

Eggplant with Onions and Cottage Cheese
*Paneer Bhare Baingan*

Cucumber in Lightly Spiced Yogurt
*Kheere Ka Raita*

Shallow-Fried Wheat Bread
*Parathe*

Chicken Curry
*Bhuna Murga*

Kidney Beans in Onion-Tomato Sauce
*Rajma*

Onion Rings in Vinegar
*Pyaz Sirkewali*

Shallow-Fried Wheat Bread
*Parathe*

---

Baked Chicken
*Masalewali Dum Murghi*

Tomatoes with Chickpeas
*Chole Bhare Tamatar*

Mung Beans with Cottage Cheese
*Moong Dal Paneerwali*

Zucchini in Yogurt
*Lauki Ka Raita*

Spinach Rice
*Palak Pullao*

Shallow-Fried Onion-Wheat Bread
*Pyaz Ke Parathe*

---

Zucchini with Dumplings
*Lauki Pakodi*

Lentils with Fenugreek
*Dal Methiwali*

Green Bell Peppers with Potatoes
*Alu Bhari Mirch*

Yogurt with Mint and Potatoes
*Podhine Alu Ka Raita*

Daikon Salad
*Mooli Ka Salat*

Pan-Broiled Wheat Bread
*Chapati*

---

Fish Curry
*Machali Kari*

Potatoes with Scallions
*Alu Pyaz Ki Sabzi*

Yogurt with Mint
*Podhine Ka Raita*

Carrot Rice
*Gajar Ka Pullao*

Egg-Filled Tortillas
*Ande Parathe*

---

Chicken in Tomato Puree
*Murgh Lajawab*

Spinach with Chickpeas
*Saag Chole*

Cucumber with Cumin
*Kheere Ka Salat*

Mushroom Rice
*Kumbhi Pullao*

Cottage Cheese-Wheat Bread
*Paneer Ki Roti*

---

Chicken with Fenugreek
*Murgh Methi*

Tomatoes with Mung Beans
*Moong Bhare Tamatar*

Mixed Vegetables in Yogurt
*Sabzi Ka Raita*

Deep-Fried Onion-Wheat Bread
*Pyaz Ki Puri*

Chicken in Sour Cream and Nuts
*Murgh Korma*

Cauliflower in Tomato-Yogurt Sauce
*Gobhi Mughlai*

Cottage Cheese in Tomato-Cashew Sauce
*Malai Kofte*

Rice with Lamb and Coriander-Mint Chutney
*Chutney Gosht Biryani*

Pan-Broiled Leavened Bread
*Naan*

---

Chicken in Coconut Milk and Peanuts
*Nariyal Ke Doodh Wala Murgh*

Cabbage with Black-Eyed Peas
*Bundgobhi Lobhiyewali*

Tomato Salad
*Khatta Meetha Salat*

Long-Grain Rice
*Saadey Chaval*

---

Lamb with Shallots
*Meat Chillifry*

Cabbage in Yogurt with Onions
*Bundgobhi Khatti*

Mixed Vegetables in Yogurt
*Sabzi Ka Raita*

Long-Grain Rice
*Saaday Chaval*

---

Lamb Chops in Tomato-Cream Sauce
*Shahi Gosht*

Potatoes with Fenugreek
*Alu Methi*

Cucumber with Cumin
*Kheere Ka Salat*

Zucchini-Wheat Bread
*Lauki Ke Parathe*

---

Chicken in Coconut Milk
*Kozhi Molee*

Lentils with Spinach
*Kire Sambhar*

Cucumber in Yogurt
*Pachadi*

Long-Grain Rice
*Saaday Chaval*

Pan-Broiled Wheat Bread
*Chapati*

---

Chicken with Spinach
*Saag Murgh*

Potatoes and Peas in Onion-Tomato Sauce
*Alu Matar*

Cucumber in Lightly Spiced Yogurt
*Kheere Ka Raita*

Pan-Broiled Wheat Bread
*Chapati*

Chicken with Mushrooms
*Murghi Sabziwali*

Eggplant in Onion-Tomato Sauce
*Bharvan Baingan Rasedar*

Potatoes in Coriander-Yogurt Sauce
*Dhaniye Ke Alu*

Mixed Vegetables in Yogurt
*Raita Sabziwala*

Tomato Chutney
*Tamatar Ki Chutney*

Deep-Fried Wheat Bread
*Puri*

---

Lamb in Coconut Milk with Coriander
and Fennel
*Meat Kari*

Chicken with Vinegar
*Murgh Vindaloo*

Mixed Vegetable Salad
*Sabzi Ka Salat*

Long-Grain Rice
*Saadey Chaval*

---

Corn Curry
*Makai Kari*

Okra with Chickpea Flour
*Bhindi Nu Shak*

Carrot Salad
*Gajar Nu Salat*

Pan-Broiled Wheat Bread
*Chapati*

---

Chicken with Yogurt and Cardamom
*Murgh Elaichi*

Beans in Fennel-Yogurt Sauce
*Sem Saunfwali*

Lamb with Yogurt
*Roghan Josh*

Tomato Salad
*Tamatar Ka Salat*

Chicken and Rice
*Kashmiri Pullao*

---

Meatballs with Mint in Onion-Yogurt Sauce
*Kofte Podhinewale*

Peas with Ginger and Cumin
*Matar Ki Ghurgri*

Mixed Vegetables in Yogurt
*Sabzi Ka Raita*

Pan-Broiled Leavened Bread
*Naan*

---

Cottage Cheese, Peas, and Nuts in Tomato Sauce
*Kaju Matar Panner*

Cucumber and Mint in Yogurt
*Kheere Podhine Ka Raita*

Pappadams
*Papad*

Rice with Chicken
*Murgh Biryani*

Lentils with Sour Cream
*Urad Malai*

Potatoes in Yogurt Sauce
*Dum Alu*

Cottage Cheese with Spinach
*Saag Paneer*

Cucumber in Lightly Spiced Yogurt
*Kheere Ka Raita*

Pan-Broiled Leavened Bread
*Naan*

Lamb with Peas
*Keema Matar*

Tomatoes with Cottage Cheese
*Paneer Bhare Tamatar*

Onions in Vinegar
*Pyaz Ka Achar*

Shallow-Fried Wheat Bread
*Parathe*

Lamb in Yogurt and Fennel
*Yakhni*

Mushrooms with Peas
*Kumbhi Matar*

Cucumber with Cumin
*Kheera Salat*

Rice with Cottage Cheese and Mint
*Podhina Paneer Biryani*

Lamb with Onions
*Gosht Do Pyaza*

Chicken with Cashew Nuts
*Malai Murghi*

Cottage Cheese and Peas
*Matar Paneer*

Cauliflower with Onions
*Gobhi Ka Keema*

Mixed Vegetable Salad
*Sabzi Ka Salat*

Rice with Mushrooms
*Kumbhi Pullao*

Deep-Fried Wheat Bread
*Puri*

Chickpeas with Onions and Tomatoes
*Chole*

Cauliflower with Onions
*Gobhi Mazedar*

Cucumber with Cumin
*Kheere Ka Salat*

Bananas in Cardamom-Flavored Yogurt
*Kele Ka Raita*

Deep-Fried Wheat Bread
*Puri*

Chicken with Coconut and Mint
*Podhina Thenga Masala Kozhi*

Green Peas
*Pacha Patani Shundal*

Onion and Cucumber Salad
*Kheere Pyaz Ka Salat*

Yogurt Rice
*Thayir Sadam*

Pan-Broiled Wheat Bread
*Chapati*

---

Lentils and Mangoes
*Dal Aamwali*

Potatoes and Green Bell Peppers
*Alu Mirch Ki Sabzi*

Chickpea and Herb Salad
*Chola Chaat*

Long-Grain Rice
*Saaday Chaval*

Spinach-Wheat Bread
*Palak Ki Roti*

---

Chicken with Yogurt and Mustard
*Murghir Kari*

Eggplant with Tomatoes and Mustard
*Sorse Begun*

Cucumber with Cumin
*Kheere Ka Salat*

Shallow-Fried Wheat Bread
*Parathe*

---

Lamb with Spices
*Attu Kari*

Eggplant with Chickpeas
*Kathrikai Kadale*

Vegetables in Yogurt
*Pachadi*

Pan-Broiled Wheat Bread
*Chapati*

---

Chicken with Herbs and Yogurt
*Sindhi Murgh*

Eggplant in Garlic-Herb Sauce
*Hare Baingan*

Mixed Vegetables in Yogurt
*Sabzi Ka Raita*

Rice with Fenugreek
*Methi Pullao*

---

Zucchini Dumplings in Onion-Tomato Sauce
*Lauki Ke Kofte*

Mung Beans with Vinegar-Soaked Spices
*Moong Sirkewali*

Tomatoes and Potatoes in Sweet-and-Sour Sauce
*Hare Tamatar Aur Alu Ki Sabzi*

Fenugreek-Wheat Bread
*Methi Ke Parathe*

Chickpeas with Cottage Cheese
*Paneer Chole*

Pumpkin with Onions and Fenugreek
*Kaddoo Ki Sabzi*

Lentil Dumplings in Yogurt
*Pakodi Ka Raita*

Sweet-and-Sour Tomato Salad
*Khatta Meetha Salat*

Tomato-Rice Casserole
*Tamatar Pullao*

Stuffed Wheat Bread
*Kachodi*

---

Rice with Kidney Beans
*Rajma Biryani*

Cucumber and Mint in Yogurt
*Kheere Podhine Ka Raita*

Pickled Limes
*Nimbu Achar*

Pappadams
*Papad*

---

Chicken with Tomatoes and Sour Cream
*Hare Tamatar Wali Murghi*

Green Bell Peppers with Vegetables
and Cottage Cheese
*Paneer Bhari Mirch*

Cucumber and Mint in Yogurt
*Kheere Podhine Ka Raita*

Mango Chutney
*Aam Ki Meethi Chutney*

Rice with Peas
*Matar Pullao*

Drinks
&
Appetizers

One of my fondest childhood memories is the eager anticipation of snacks that were sure to come when I accompanied my parents on visits to friends' homes. There would be flaky *samosas* with spicy potato filling, which I loved, *pakoras* hot from the karhai served with fragrant coriander chutney, and to wash it all down would be cool ginger-flavored lime juice or tea spiced with cardamom.

In India, *pakoras*, *vadas*, *samosas*, and other savories are featured mainly at teatime as snacks rather than before dinner as appetizers. The chutneys, relishes, and pickles accompanying them not only serve as dips for the snacks but also appear at the dinner table to add zest to the food. A traditional Indian meal, in fact, is rarely preceded by an appetizer except in the form of a drink or sherbet (which in India means a sugar syrup-based drink). This trend is now changing, however, with more and more people traveling abroad and incorporating Western food habits into their life-styles. Items from this chapter, as well as from the barbecue chapter, are now apt to be served before dinner or as light meals in themselves.

# Lime Juice with Ginger
## *Shikanji Adrakwali*

Here, lime juice is enlivened with a dash of ginger. This form of limeade is very popular in many parts of India during the summer months. The concentrate can be made ahead of time and refrigerated until use. Just add water when you are ready to serve.

4 cups cold water
1 tablespoon freshly grated ginger
1/2 teaspoon *kala namak* (black salt, optional)
6 to 7 tablespoons sugar
2 limes
Crushed ice

In a jug, mix the water, ginger, kala namak, and sugar. Extract the juice from the limes and add to the jug. Mix well and let stand in the refrigerator for 30 minutes. Strain the juice and serve over crushed ice.

Yield: Four 8-ounce glasses.

# Almond Milk
## *Thandai*

Visits to my grandmother's home were eagerly anticipated because she always kept a jug of this delicious drink in her refrigerator.

15 almonds
3/4 cup water
8 cardamom pods
1 tablespoon fennel seeds
10 peppercorns
1 teaspoon white poppy seeds
1 1/4 cups milk
3 to 4 tablespoons sugar
Crushed ice

Soak the almonds overnight in cold water. Drain and place them in the container of a blender along with 1/4 cup of the water; blend to a smooth paste. Grind seeds from the cardamom pods along with the fennel, peppercorns, and poppy seeds, then soak in the remaining 1/2 cup water for 1 hour or more. Strain this liquid through 3 folds of cheesecloth. Add the almond paste, milk, and sugar. Mix well and serve over crushed ice.

Yield: Two to three 8-ounce glasses.

# Sweetened Yogurt Drink
## *Lassi*

A popular summertime drink, *lassi* is sold in numerous stalls that dot the bazaars of northern India. It is, however, not just poured into a glass. It has to be transferred over and over from one glass to the other, the first sometimes held at a height of 2 feet. This gives it the all-important froth; without it, no glass of lassi would be complete. I find it much easier to achieve similar results with an electric blender.

**1 cup plain yogurt**
**1 cup cold water**
**2 to 3 drops *kewra* or rose essence**
**3 to 4 tablespoons sugar**
**Crushed ice**

Place all the ingredients except the ice in the container of a blender and blend at high speed until the mixture becomes frothy (about 1 minute). Serve in tall glasses over crushed ice.

Yield: Two to three 8-ounce glasses.

# Spicy Yogurt Drink
## *Namkeen Lassi*

In many Indian homes this lassi forms part of the midday meal. Considered to have great therapeutic value, it is served especially to convalescents.

**1 cup plain yogurt**
**1 cup cold water**
**Salt, to taste**
**1/4 teaspoon cayenne pepper**
**1/4 to 1/2 teaspoon *kala namak* (black salt)**
**1/2 teaspoon ground roasted cumin seeds**

Place all the ingredients in the container of a blender and blend at high speed for 1 minute. Chill and serve in tall glasses.

Yield: Two 8-ounce glasses.

# Yogurt Drink with Mango
## *Lassi Aamwali*

This is a slight variation of lassi. Mango pulp adds a new dimension to its flavor.

**1 cup plain yogurt**
**2 cups cold water**
**6 tablespoons canned mango pulp**
**3 to 4 tablespoons sugar**
**3 to 4 drops *kewra* or rose essence**
**Crushed ice**

Place all the ingredients except the ice in the container of a blender and blend at high speed until the mixture becomes frothy (about 1 minute). Serve in tall glasses over crushed ice.

Yield: Two to three 8-ounce glasses.

# Tangy Mango Juice
## *Khatta Pana*

Unripe mangoes are used widely in Indian cuisine for making sherbets (cold drinks), pickles, and chutneys. Most Indian grocery stores in the United States stock these mangoes during the summer. They are extremely sour, with a flavor not easily forgotten. Choose unblemished green mangoes that are hard and unyielding to the touch.

**1 teaspoon vegetable oil, for rubbing mango**
**1 large unripe green mango (about 1 pound)**
**3 cups water**
**Salt, to taste**
**1/4 teaspoon cayenne pepper**
**3/4 teaspoon *kala namak* (black salt)**
**1 teaspoon ground roasted cumin seeds**
**1/2 teaspoon ground fennel seeds**
**Mint leaves, chopped, for garnish**

Rub a little oil over the mango and either bake it in a 400°F oven until tender (about 40 minutes) or grill it over a charcoal fire until tender. Remove and discard the skin and the seed and scrape away all the pulp. Place the pulp and all the remaining ingredients except the mint in the container of a blender and blend at high speed for 1 minute. Chill the juice, strain it, and serve in tall glasses. Garnish with chopped mint.

Yield: Four 8-ounce glasses.

# Mango Juice with Cantaloupe
## *Pana Kharbuzewala*

A jug of this popular drink is always kept ready during the summer months when the heat in India can be scorching. This drink helps cool the body and revive flagging spirits. Chopped cantaloupe, not traditionally added to the juice, was my mother's successful idea.

**1 large unripe green mango (about 1 pound)**
**3 cups water**
**7 to 8 tablespoons sugar**
**2 slices cantaloupe**
**Crushed ice**

Place the mango in a saucepan with enough water to cover. Boil until tender. Let cool, remove the skin and the seed, and scrape away all the pulp. Place the pulp, the 3 cups water, and sugar in the container of a blender and blend at high speed for 1 minute. Transfer the contents to a jug and refrigerate until ready to use. Strain the juice before serving. Chop the cantaloupe slices into small bits and stir into the mango juice. Serve in tall glasses over crushed ice.

Yield: Four 8-ounce glasses.

# Tomato Soup
## *Rasam*

This soup is included in every South Indian meal. It can also be served as an appetizer and fits well in a Western meal as a spicy first course.

1/4 cup *tur dal* (yellow lentils)
1 1/2 cups water
2 pounds tomatoes
3 cloves garlic
1/2-inch piece fresh ginger
10 to 12 dried curry leaves
Pinch crushed asafoetida
1/2 teaspoon black peppercorns, crushed coarsely
Salt, to taste
1/4 teaspoon cayenne pepper
1/2 teaspoon ground turmeric
1/2 teaspoon ground cumin seeds
1/4 teaspoon ground coriander seeds
1/2 teaspoon tamarind paste *or* 1 tablespoon
    lemon juice
1 tablespoon vegetable oil
1/4 teaspoon whole cumin seeds
1/2 teaspoon black mustard seeds

Wash the lentils well, place them and 1/2 cup of the water in a large heavy-bottomed saucepan, and let soak for 30 minutes. Meanwhile, chop the tomatoes coarsely and grate the garlic and ginger. Cook the lentils with their soaking liquid over low heat until tender (about 25 minutes). When soft, add the tomatoes, garlic, ginger, 8 curry leaves, asafoetida, black pepper, salt, cayenne, tumeric, ground cumin seeds, coriander, and tamarind paste. Partially cover the pan and cook for 20 minutes longer. Let cool, then strain the liquid through a sieve into another large pan, squeezing the pulp well. Add the remaining 1 cup water to this liquid and simmer for 5 minutes. In a small pan heat the oil and add the whole cumin seeds, mustard seeds, and remaining curry leaves. When the seeds splutter, pour the oil into the soup. Mix well and serve hot.

Yield: Serves 4.

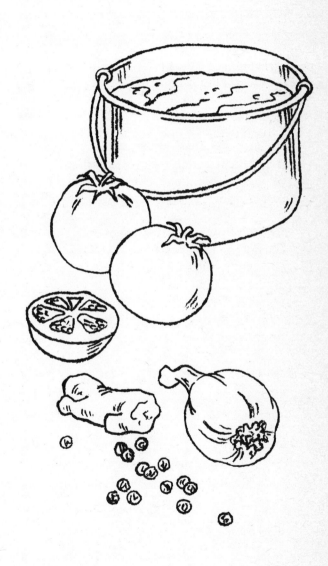

# Onion Rings

## *Pyaz Ke Pakore*

Anyone who likes onion rings will enjoy this zesty Indian version. Thin rounds of potato, eggplant, or zucchini could be used in place of onions.

2 large onions
3/4 cup chickpea flour
1/2 cup water
Salt, to taste
1/4 teaspoon cayenne pepper
1/2 teaspoon cumin seeds
2 tablespoons lemon juice
Vegetable oil, for deep-frying

Peel the onions, slice them into rounds of medium thickness, and separate into rings. Make a smooth batter with the chickpea flour and the water. Add the salt, cayenne, cumin, and lemon juice. Heat the oil for deep-frying over medium-high heat. Dip the onion rings into the batter and slide them into the hot oil. Reduce the heat to medium and fry until the onion rings are golden on all sides. Drain on paper towels and serve hot.

Yield: Serves 4.

# Potatoes in Puff Pastry

## *Samose*

Using puff pastry for the *samose* shells makes the preparation of this dish much easier. I have also devised attractive little samose morsels instead of the larger more traditional version. They go very well with tomato chutney or tamarind-mint chutney.

2 large potatoes
1 medium plus 1 small onion
3/4-inch piece fresh ginger
3 tablespoons vegetable oil
1/2 teaspoon cumin seeds
Tiny pinch crushed asafoetida (optional)
Salt, to taste
1/2 teaspoon *garam masala*
1/2 teaspoon ground coriander seeds
1/4 teaspoon cayenne pepper
2 tablespoons lemon juice
2 frozen puff pastry sheets (1 pound, 1 1/4 ounces)
1 egg, beaten

Boil the potatoes until tender, then peel and chop coarsely and set aside. Chop the onions very finely. Grate the ginger. In a large heavy-bottomed skillet over medium heat, warm the oil. Add the cumin and asafoetida (if used). Wait a moment and then add the grated ginger. Cook for 1 minute, then add the chopped onions. Saute until well browned (12 to 15 minutes). Reduce the heat and add the salt, *garam masala*, coriander, and cayenne. Mix well, then add the mashed potatoes. Saute for 2 to 3 minutes and remove from heat. Mix in the lemon juice.

Thaw the puff pastry sheets according to the package directions. Divide each sheet into 3 equal strips. Roll out the strips lightly on a floured board, then divide each strip into 4 equal squares.

Preheat the oven to 350°F. Place a teaspoonful of the potato filling in the center of each square. Fold one edge of the pastry over the filling to form a triangle. If that is hard to manage, you may form rectangles. Press the edges together to seal. Place on a greased baking sheet and brush with the beaten egg. Bake uncovered until the tops are golden (about 25 minutes).

Yield: 24 samosas.

# Dumplings with Spinach and Black-Eyed Peas

## *Palak Lobhive Ke Vade*

This unusual dish, contributed by my friend Revathy, will have everyone guessing at the ingredients. Serve these *vadas* with any chutney of your choice. They may be fried a few hours ahead of time and warmed in the oven before serving. For variety, try substituting mustard greens for the spinach.

1 cup dried black-eyed peas
5 ounces frozen chopped spinach
2 to 3 tablespoons water
1 medium onion
1 teaspoon finely chopped fresh ginger
1/2 teaspoon cumin seeds
1/2 teaspoon cayenne pepper
Salt, to taste
Vegetable oil, for deep-frying

Soak the black-eyed peas overnight in enough water to cover. Thaw the spinach, squeeze out excess water, and set aside. Drain the peas and grind finely in a blender or food processor with the water. Chop the onion finely. In a large bowl mix the spinach, ground black-eyed peas, chopped onion, ginger, cumin, cayenne, and salt.

Warm the oil for deep-frying over medium-high heat. Wetting your hands lightly whenever necessary, shape balls 1 1/2 inches in diameter from the spinach-pea mixture. Flatten each ball slightly with your palms and drop it gently into the hot oil. Reduce the heat to medium and fry the vadas until golden on all sides. Drain on paper towels and serve hot.

Yield: Serves 4.

# Potato and Tomato Dumplings

## *Alu Tamatar Ke Pakore*

These dumplings are a delicious accompaniment to cocktails. Serve hot with tomato or coriander chutney. You can also add these to spiced yogurt (see any raita recipe).

4 medium potatoes
1 large firm tomato
1/4 teaspoon ground roasted cumin seeds
1/4 teaspoon whole cumin seeds
Salt, to taste
1/4 teaspoon cayenne pepper
3 tablespoons chickpea flour
Vegetable oil, for deep-frying

Boil the potatoes until tender, then peel and mash coarsely. Chop the tomato finely. In a large bowl mix the mashed potatoes, ground cumin, whole cumin seeds, salt, cayenne, and chickpea flour. Gently mix in the chopped tomato.

Warm the oil for deep-frying over medium-high heat. Using your hands shape balls 1 1/2 inches in diameter from the potato mixture. Drop them gently into the hot oil, reduce the heat to medium, and deep-fry the dumplings until golden on all sides. Drain on paper towels and serve hot.

Yield: Serves 4.

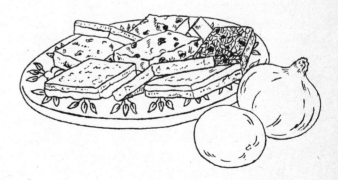

# Corn Dumplings

## *Bhutte Ke Pakore*

Deliciously soft on the inside, brown and crisp on the outside, these *pakoras* are a corn lover's dream. The recipe was given to me by my sister-in-law Mamta, a truly versatile cook.

**1 1/2 cups whole corn kernels (fresh, canned, or frozen)**
**1 cup water**
**1 medium onion**
**1/4-inch piece fresh ginger (optional)**
**1 teaspoon chopped fresh coriander leaves (optional)**
**2 tablespoons flour**
**Salt, to taste**
**1/2 teaspoon cumin seeds**
**1/4 teaspoon *garam masala***
**Vegetable oil, for deep-frying**

Cook the corn in the water for 8 minutes over high heat. Drain, let cool slightly, then grind finely in a food processor or blender. Transfer to a large bowl and set aside. Finely chop the onion and ginger (if used). Add to the ground corn along with the coriander (if used), flour, salt, cumin, and *garam masala*. Mix well.

Warm the oil for deep-frying over medium-high heat. Lightly wetting your hands whenever necessary, shape small balls, no bigger than 1 1/2 inches in diameter, from the corn mixture. Drop them gently into the hot oil. Reduce the heat to medium-low and fry the dumplings until golden brown on all sides. Drain on absorbent paper and serve hot.

Yield: Serves 4.

# Dumplings with Zucchini and Mint

## *Podhine Lauki Ke Pakore*

The fresh flavors of mint and coriander make these *pakoras* wonderfully fragrant. Line a basket attractively with sprigs of mint and arrange the pakoras on top. Serve lots of your favorite chutney on the side.

**2 medium zucchini (about 1 1/4 pounds total)**
**1 large onion**
**1 cup fresh mint leaves**
**1/4 cup fresh coriander leaves**
**1 cup crumbled homemade cottage cheese**
**Salt, to taste**
**1/4 teaspoon cayenne pepper**
**1/2 cup chickpea flour**
**Vegetable oil, for deep-frying**

Peel the zucchini and grate in a food processor. Gently squeeze out the excess water with your hands, and set aside. Chop the onion finely. Chop the mint and coriander leaves. In a medium bowl mix all the ingredients except the vegetable oil.

Warm the oil for deep-frying over medium-high heat. Using your hands shape balls 1 1/2 inches in diameter from the zucchini mixture. Drop them gently into the hot oil, putting in as many as the pan can hold in a single layer. Reduce the heat to medium and fry the dumplings until golden on all sides. Drain on paper towels and serve hot.

Yield: Serves 4.

# Dumplings with Bread, Nuts, and Yogurt

## *Bread Aur Dahi Ke Pakore*

These *pakoras* can be deep-fried a few hours before you intend to serve them. Keep them wrapped in aluminum foil and warm them in the oven when ready to serve. They go well with catsup or any chutney.

2/3 cup plain yogurt
1/2 cup water
Salt, to taste
1/4 teaspoon cayenne pepper
4 slices whole wheat or white bread
1/2 cup roasted peanuts *or* 1/4 cup roasted
   peanuts and 1/4 cup roasted cashew nuts
1 medium onion
1/4 cup chickpea flour
Vegetable oil, for deep-frying

Beat the yogurt and 1/4 cup of the water together until smooth. Add the salt and cayenne. Break the slices of bread into small pieces and soak in the yogurt mixture for 5 to 7 minutes. Grind the nuts coarsely. Chop the onion finely. Add the nuts and chopped onion to the bread-yogurt mixture. Stir in the chickpea flour. Add the remaining 1/4 cup water and make into a batter. Leave little lumps of bread in the batter; do not make it too smooth.

Warm the oil for deep-frying over medium-high heat and gently drop in rounded tablespoons of the batter. Reduce the heat to medium and fry the dumplings until golden on all sides. Drain on paper towels and serve hot.

Yield: Serves 4.

# Fried Peanuts

## *Besan Ki Moongphali*

Peanuts coated with a spicy batter, then deep-fried until brown and crisp, are an unusual snack from the Kerala region in South India. You could also add these peanuts to salads for a spicy, crunchy effect.

1 cup raw unskinned peanuts
Salt, to taste
1/4 to 1/2 teaspoon cayenne pepper
1/2 teaspoon ground turmeric
1/2 teaspoon cumin seeds
Pinch baking powder
3 tablespoons chickpea flour
2 tablespoons lemon juice
Vegetable oil, for deep-frying

Place the peanuts in a small bowl and sprinkle with salt, cayenne, turmeric, cumin, baking powder, and chickpea flour. Mix well, then add the lemon juice and mix in with your fingers. The batter should be stiff and cling to the peanuts.

Warm the oil for deep-frying over medium-high heat. When the oil begins to smoke slightly, reduce the heat to low and sprinkle in the peanuts. (Frying over low heat is important to ensure crispness.) Separate peanuts as much as possible with a spatula and fry until the batter turns golden. Remove the peanuts with a slotted spoon and drain on paper towels. Allow them to cool completely at room temperature before storing them in an airtight container.

Yield: About 1 cup peanuts.

# Ground Lamb Kebabs
## *Shami Kabab*

In Indian cuisine kebabs are made with ground meat or cubed meat threaded onto skewers. You can make the kebabs a few hours ahead of time and warm them in the oven before serving. Leftover Shami Kabab makes an excellent lunch when stuffed in pita bread pockets or enclosed in a roll with lettuce and tomato—burger style. Serve this dish for dinner in a sauce of your choice.

**1/3 cup *chana dal* (yellow split peas)**
**1 cup water**
**1 pound ground lamb or beef**
**8 whole cloves**
**1 teaspoon peppercorns**
**5 cardamom pods**
**1/2-inch stick cinnamon**
**2 bay leaves**
**1 dried red chilli (deseeded, if desired)**
**Salt, to taste**
**1/2-inch piece fresh ginger**
**1 large egg**
**8 tablespoons vegetable oil**

Wash the split peas well, place them and the water in a large heavy-bottomed saucepan, and let soak for 1 hour.

Add the lamb, cloves, peppercorns, cardamom, cinnamon, bay leaves, chilli, salt, and ginger. Cover and bring to a boil, then reduce the heat to very low and cook covered for 45 minutes. Uncover, increase the heat to high, and boil off the remaining liquid while stirring (about 10 minutes). Let cool slightly, then grind to a fine paste in a food processor or blender. No whole spices should remain. Transfer to a bowl, stir in the egg, and mix well.

In a large heavy-bottomed or nonstick skillet over medium heat, warm the oil. Shape balls about

1 1/2 inches in diameter from the lamb mixture and drop them gently into the hot oil. Reduce the heat to medium-low and fry the kebabs until brown on all sides. Drain and serve hot.

Yield: Serves 4.

# Pappadams
## *Papad*

The delicious crunch of these popular crisp lentil wafers has brightened up many a meal. The fragile disks are available in all Indian grocery stores. They are made from a paste of ground lentils seasoned with black pepper, garlic, or cumin seeds. To cook *pappadams*, you may deep-fry them in hot oil or roast them over a flame. You can halve them if they seem too large to handle.

Since pappadams cook quickly, when I give a party and find myself running late, I heap pappadam quarters in a basket and serve them as appetizers. They wet the appetite for the food to follow.

For deep-frying, warm vegetable oil over medium heat and slide in the pappadams. They will be cooked in seconds, so you have to remove them quickly. Use tongs or a slotted spoon. Do not let them burn—the color of cooked pappadams should not be very different from dried ones. Allow 2 to 3 halves per person.

To heat pappadams over a gas flame, grip a corner of the pappadam with tongs. Hold a portion of it 1/2 inch over a low flame, until it begins to bubble slightly and change color. Watch carefully for signs of burning. Expose the remaining portions of the pappadam to the flame little by little, until all of it is heated.

# Main Dishes: Lamb or Beef

I had my first taste of nonvegetarian food at the age of sixteen, when I left home to attend college. Growing up in a strict vegetarian family, we were never allowed to eat meat at home. Once out of my parents' reach, I warily tasted the meat and chicken dishes served in the college dining room, and from there went on to sample every kind of meat preparation that Delhi had to offer. I tasted Delhi's famous Mughlai cuisine, Andhra's fiery hot chilli chicken, Punjab's rich mutton curries, Goa's seafood preparations, and Kerala's coconut milk-based molees.

Although a large majority of India's population is vegetarian, over the centuries Moghul and European invaders have left their mark, so that now there is a sizable Moslem and Christian population who eat meat. Even among Hindus, increasing Western influence has made meat eating more common. A friend who eats beef only when traveling abroad insists that it is all right to eat it as long as the cows aren't Indian. Even vegetarianism is open to a wide variety of interpretations among Indians; some eat eggs, others only chicken or seafood, and still others, such as my mother, who will not even eat cake or ice cream since they contain eggs. Assamese brahmins who consider themselves strict vegetarians eat fish, which they think of as a vegetable.

Goat meat, or mutton as it is known in India, is eaten extensively. Because chicken is more expensive than goat meat it is not used as much. Seafood is abundant in India's coastal waters, and places such as Kerala, Goa, and Bengal are famous for their seafood preparations. The next three chapters have recipes from all over India. A point to remember when cooking lamb—weigh it only after boning and defatting it. If you like, you can leave the bones in, as most Indians do, but it is certainly easier to eat the meat when it is boneless. You can substitute beef for lamb in all the following recipes.

# Lamb with Onions and Spices

## *Gosht Masalewala*

1 pound boned and defatted lamb or beef
2 medium onions
1-inch piece fresh ginger
6 cloves garlic
2 medium tomatoes, coarsely chopped or 3 tablespoons plain yogurt
1/2 teaspoon ground turmeric
Salt, to taste
1/4 teaspoon cayenne pepper
1 teaspoon ground coriander seeds
2 tablespoons vegetable oil
1 teaspoon ground cumin seeds
4 cardamom pods
1-inch stick cinnamon
4 whole cloves
1 bay leaf
3/4 teaspoon *garam masala*

Cut the lamb into 1-inch pieces. Place the onions, ginger, garlic, and tomatoes (if used) in the container of a blender and blend to a smooth paste. Transfer to a large bowl. Add the turmeric, salt, cayenne, and coriander. If you use yogurt, add it now. Marinate the meat in this paste for 1 hour or more at room temperature.

In a large heavy-bottomed saucepan over medium heat, warm the oil. Add the cumin, cardamom, cinnamon, cloves, and bay leaf. When the spices darken (1 to 2 seconds), add the meat and all its marinade. Cover, increase the heat to high, and bring the contents of the pan to a boil. Reduce the heat to low, cover, and cook until the lamb is tender and the sauce is thick, dark, and clinging to the meat (about 1 hour), stirring occasionally. Add a sprinkling of water if the sauce sticks to the bottom of the pan. Add the *garam masala* and serve.

Yield: Serves 4 with other dishes.

# Lamb with Onions

## *Gosht Do Pyaza*

In this dish, one batch of onions is minced, sauteed, and cooked with the lamb; the other is thinly sliced, sauteed, and folded in toward the end of cooking. This is an elegant dish, suitable for dinner parties. It is also good stuffed into pita bread pockets and topped with a little raita.

1 pound boned and defatted lamb or beef
2 large onions
7 tablespoons vegetable oil
3/4-inch piece fresh ginger
4 large cloves garlic
1 bay leaf
2 whole cloves
1/2-inch stick cinnamon
1/2 teaspoon cumin seeds
1/2 teaspoon ground roasted cumin seeds
1/2 teaspoon ground coriander seeds
1/4 teaspoon cayenne pepper
Salt, to taste
6 tablespoons plain yogurt
1/4 cup water
1/2 teaspoon *garam masala*

Cut the lamb into 1-inch pieces and set aside. Peel and slice 1 onion into thin half rounds. In a large heavy-bottomed saucepan over medium heat, warm 5 tablespoons of the oil. Saute the sliced onion until dark brown (about 15 minutes). Remove with a slotted spoon, leaving as much oil in the pan as possible, and spread on a paper towel to drain. Place the other onion, ginger, and garlic in the container of a food processor or blender and mince.

Add the remaining 2 tablespoons oil to the pan and warm over medium heat. Add the bay leaf, cloves, cinnamon, and cumin seeds. When the spices darken (1 to 2 seconds), add the minced onion mixture and saute until lightly browned (7 to 8 minutes). Add the ground roasted cumin seeds, coriander, cayenne, and salt. Saute for 1 minute. Beat the yogurt with a spoon and stir it in. Cook for 2 minutes. Add the lamb and the water. Cover, reduce the heat to low, and cook until the lamb is tender (about 1 hour), stirring occasionally. Mix in the sauteed onions and *garam masala*. Serve hot.

Yield: Serves 4 with other dishes.

# Ground Lamb with Peas

## *Keema Matar*

This popular dish from North India is often used as a stuffing for green bell peppers, eggplant, zucchini, or tomatoes, which are then baked in the oven. It can also be stuffed into Shallow-Fried Wheat Bread, combined with rice and formed into a delicious *biryani*, or served on French bread topped with grated Cheddar cheese and grilled in the oven. As a variation you can also add chopped spinach or crumbled homemade cottage cheese to the sauce along with the lamb. It also makes a tasty meal when served simply with rice and a salad.

**2 medium onions**
**1/2-inch piece fresh ginger**
**4 cloves garlic**
**2 tablespoons vegetable oil**
**1 teaspoon cumin seeds**
**1/2-inch stick cinnamon**
**1 bay leaf**
**2 medium tomatoes, chopped coarsely**
**3 tablespoons plain yogurt**
**Salt, to taste**
**1/4 teaspoon cayenne pepper**
**1 teaspoon ground coriander seeds**
**1/2 teaspoon ground turmeric**
**1 pound lean ground lamb or beef**
**1/4 cup water**
**1 cup green peas (fresh or frozen)**
**1 teaspoon *garam masala***

Chop the onions finely. Grate the ginger and garlic. In a large heavy-bottomed saucepan over medium heat, warm the oil. Add the cumin, cinnamon, and bay leaf. When the spices darken (1 to 2 seconds), add the grated ginger and garlic. Cook for 1 minute, then add the chopped onions and saute until browned (about 10 minutes). Add the toma-toes and cook until soft (about 5 minutes). Beat the yogurt with a spoon until smooth and add it gradually, stirring constantly. Cook for another 5 minutes. Add the salt, cayenne, coriander, and turmeric. Add the lamb and stir to mix with the spices. Add the water and peas, cover, reduce the heat to low, and cook until the lamb is tender (about 40 minutes), stirring occasionally. Mix in the *garam masala* and serve.

Yield: Serves 4 with other dishes.

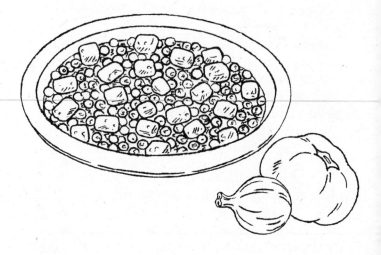

# Lamb with Spices
## *Attu Kari*

To many people, Madras food is synonymous with hot and spicy dishes. Although the heat can be adjusted to personal taste, the spices (predominantly coriander and black pepper) give the unique Madras flavor. Tamarind rather than tomatoes or yogurt is generally used to add sourness to the dish. This curry is a good illustration of the cuisine of this region.

1 1/2 pounds boned and defatted lamb or beef
1 1/2 teaspoons ground coriander seeds
1 teaspoon ground cumin seeds
1/4 teaspoon cayenne pepper
Salt, to taste
2 teaspoons freshly ground black pepper
2 tablespoons plus 1 cup water
2 medium onions
1/2-inch piece fresh ginger
4 tablespoons vegetable oil
1-inch stick cinnamon
1 bay leaf
1 teaspoon black mustard seeds
10 dried curry leaves
1 teaspoon tamarind paste *or* 1 tablespoon lemon
  juice
8 cardamom pods, seeds removed and ground

Dry the meat with a paper towel and cut it into 1/2-inch cubes. In a large bowl combine the coriander, cumin, cayenne, salt, and black pepper. Add the 2 tablespoons water and make a paste, then rub it into the cubes of meat and let marinate at room temperature for 30 minutes. Slice the onions into thin half rounds. Grate the ginger.

In a large heavy-bottomed, preferably nonstick saucepan over medium heat, warm the oil. Add the cinnamon, bay leaf, mustard seeds, and curry leaves.

As soon as the seeds begin to splutter, add the grated ginger. Cook for 1 minute, then add the sliced onions and saute until lightly browned (7 to 8 minutes). Add the cubes of meat along with all accumulated juices and spices, and sear for 5 minutes. Reduce the heat to low, add the 1 cup water and the tamarind paste (if using lemon juice add it just before serving). Cover and cook until the lamb is tender (about 45 minutes), stirring occasionally. If the sauce is too thin, boil it down until it clings to the meat. Add the ground cardamom and lemon juice, if using, and serve hot.

Yield: Serves 4 with other dishes.

# Lamb in Herb and Butter Sauce

## *Makhani Gosht*

The lamb is fried in butter toward the end of the cooking period, giving it a rich buttery flavor and a reddish fried look. If you find the dish too fatty, you may cut down on the amount of butter or omit frying in butter entirely.

**1 pound boned and defatted lamb or beef**
**2 medium onions**
**2 tablespoons vegetable oil**
**1-inch piece fresh ginger**
**4 cloves garlic**
**1/2 cup water**
**2 tablespoons plain yogurt**
**1 teaspoon ground coriander seeds**
**1 teaspoon ground cumin seeds**
**Salt, to taste**
**1/4 teaspoon cayenne pepper**
**1/2 teaspoon ground turmeric**
**4 tablespoons butter**
**1 teaspoon *garam masala***
**1/4 cup fresh mint leaves, chopped**
**1/4 cup fresh coriander leaves, chopped**
**2 tablespoons lemon juice**

Cut the lamb into 1-inch cubes. Slice 1 onion into thin half rounds. In a large heavy-bottomed saucepan over medium heat, warm the oil. Saute the sliced onion until well browned (about 12 minutes). Lift out of the oil with a slotted spoon and set aside, reserving the oil in the pan. Place the remaining onion, ginger, garlic, and the water in the container of a food processor and blend to a fine paste. Transfer to a large bowl and add the yogurt, ground coriander seeds, cumin, salt, cayenne, and turmeric. Add the lamb to this paste and marinate for 1 hour or more at room temperature.

Warm the oil remaining in the pan over medium heat and add the meat with all its marinade. Reduce the heat to low and cook covered until the lamb is tender (about 1 hour), adding more water if necessary and stirring occasionally to prevent burning. Uncover the pan and increase the heat to high. Add the butter and boil down the sauce, stirring often. The sauce should cling to the meat at the end of the cooking time, and the meat should take on a fried reddish look. Fold in the reserved sauteed onions and the *garam masala*. Remove the pan from the heat, mix in the fresh mint and coriander leaves and lemon juice, and serve.

Yield: Serves 4 with other dishes.

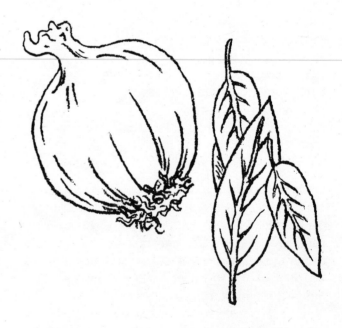

# Lamb with Yogurt

## *Roghan Josh*

This dish gets its rich red appearance from paprika, which is used extensively in Kashmiri cooking. It is an exquisite dish, eminently suitable for dinner parties. You could serve it with Spinach with Cottage Cheese and Pan-Broiled Leavened Bread, or stuff it into pita bread pockets topped with a little raita.

1 pound boned and defatted lamb or beef
1 large onion
2 tablespoons vegetable oil
1/2-inch stick cinnamon
2 whole cloves
8 cardamom pods
1 bay leaf
3 tablespoons paprika (preferably Hungarian)
Salt, to taste
1/4 teaspoon cayenne pepper
1/2 teaspoon ground ginger
1/4 cup plain yogurt
1/2 cup water
3/4 teaspoon *garam masala*

Dry the meat with a paper towel and cut it into 1-inch cubes. Slice the onion into thin half rounds. In a large heavy-bottomed saucepan over medium heat, warm the oil. Add the cinnamon, cloves, 2 cardamom pods, and bay leaf. When the spices puff up and darken, add the sliced onion and lamb. Cook until they have browned lightly and the liquid they have given off has evaporated (about 15 minutes). Add the paprika, salt, cayenne, and ginger. Cook for 2 minutes. Beat the yogurt with a spoon until smooth. Reduce the heat to low and mix in the yogurt. Increase the heat to medium and cook for 5 minutes. Add the water and 1/2 teaspoon of the *garam masala*. Cover, reduce the heat to low, and cook until the lamb is tender and a thick sauce clings to the meat (about 45 minutes), stirring occasionally to prevent burning.

Remove the seeds from the remaining 6 cardamom pods, grind the seeds, and add them to the pan along with the remaining 1/4 teaspoon *garam masala*. Serve hot.

Yield: Serves 4 with other dishes.

# Meatballs with Mint in Onion-Yogurt Sauce

## *Kofte Podhinewale*

The ancient technique of sealing precooked food and letting it mellow in its own juices and sauces over low heat is known as *dum*. This style of cooking originated in 1784 when the ruler Asaf-Ud-Daulah ordered food to be cooked in large quantities for his work force. Meats, vegetables, yogurt, and spices were combined in huge pots, which were then sealed and placed over gentle coal fires all night. Food cooked in this way tasted good and the procedure was soon refined for use in the royal kitchens. The sauce for this dish may be made ahead of time and kept frozen or refrigerated until use.

1/2-inch piece fresh ginger
1 green chilli
1 cup fresh mint leaves
1 pound lean ground lamb or beef
1/2 teaspoon salt
2 medium onions
4 large cloves garlic
3 tablespoons vegetable oil
1/2 teaspoon cumin seeds
1 bay leaf
1/2-inch stick cinnamon
1/2 teaspoon ground turmeric
1/2 teaspoon ground coriander seeds
Salt, to taste
5 tablespoons plain yogurt
1 teaspoon *garam masala*
1/2 cup water

Mince the ginger, chilli, and mint in the container of a food processor or blender. Transfer to a large bowl, add the lamb and salt, and mix well.

Preheat the oven to 450°F. Using your hands, shape balls about 1 1/2 inches in diameter from the lamb mixture. Place them in a single layer in an ovenproof dish and bake uncovered for 30 minutes. Turn off the oven, remove the dish, and drain off and discard all the fat. Set aside.

Meanwhile, in the container of a food processor or blender, mince the onions and garlic together. In a small heavy-bottomed saucepan over medium heat, warm the oil. Add the cumin, bay leaf, and cinnamon. When the spices darken (1 to 2 seconds), add the minced onions and garlic and cook until well browned (about 15 minutes). Reduce the heat to low, add the turmeric, coriander, and salt, and cook for 1 minute. Beat the yogurt with a spoon and mix it in, stirring constantly. Cook for 10 minutes, then mix in the *garam masala* and the water. Remove from the heat.

Preheat the oven to 250°F. Pour the sauce evenly over the reserved meatballs, cover tightly with aluminum foil, and bake for 15 minutes. Serve hot.

Yield: Serves 4 with other dishes.

# Lamb with Shallots

## *Meat Chillifry*

This spicy stew is ideal for cold winter evenings. It could be served with rice, Pan-Broiled Leavened Bread or French bread.

1 1/2 pounds boned and defatted lamb or beef
1/2 teaspoon salt, or more if needed
1/2 cup distilled white vinegar
1/2-inch stick cinnamon
4 whole cloves
4 cardamom pods
1/2 teaspoon peppercorns
1 dried red chilli (optional)
1 teaspoon coriander seeds
1/2 teaspoon cumin seeds
1/4 teaspoon fenugreek seeds
1 tablespoon unsweetened desiccated coconut
  powder
1-inch piece fresh ginger
2 tablespoons vegetable oil
1 teaspoon black mustard seeds
8 to 10 dried curry leaves
1/2 pound shallots, peeled
1 large tomato, chopped coarsely
1/4 cup water, if needed

Cut the lamb into 1-inch cubes. In a large bowl combine the salt and vinegar, add the lamb, and let marinate for 30 minutes at room temperature. Meanwhile, in a small heavy-bottomed skillet over low heat, dry-roast together the cinnamon, cloves, cardamom, peppercorns, chilli, coriander, cumin, fenugreek, and coconut. Let cool, then grind. Grate the ginger.

Warm the oil over medium heat in a heavy-bottomed saucepan. Add the mustard seeds and curry leaves. Wait 1 to 2 seconds, then add the grated ginger and the whole shallots. Saute for 5 minutes. Lift the meat pieces out of the vinegar mixture and add to the pan (discard the vinegar). Cook until they are browned (about 5 minutes). Add the tomato and the ground roasted spices. Cover, reduce the heat to low, and cook until the lamb is tender (about 1 hour), adding the water if the sauce seems too dry or sticks to the pan. Adjust salt before serving.

Yield: Serves 4 with other dishes.

# Lamb Chops in Tomato-Cream Sauce

## *Shahi Gosht*

This rich dish is ideal for parties, because it is easy to prepare and is sure to impress the most discriminating palate. Serve it with Potatoes in Creamy Yogurt Sauce and Pan-Broiled Leavened Bread.

**1 teaspoon ground coriander seeds**
**1/2 teaspoon ground cumin seeds**
**1/2 teaspoon freshly ground black pepper**
**1/4 teaspoon cayenne pepper**
**Salt, to taste**
**1/4 teaspoon ground turmeric**
**1 1/2 teaspoons water**
**2 lamb chops (3/4 to 1 pound total), defatted, or beef**
**8 almonds**
**1/4 cup whipping cream**
**1 medium onion**
**1/2-inch piece fresh ginger**
**4 cloves garlic**
**2 tablespoons vegetable oil**
**1/2 teaspoon cumin seeds**
**1 1/4 cups canned crushed tomatoes in thick puree**
**1 teaspoon ground fennel seeds**

In a large bowl combine the coriander, cumin, black pepper, cayenne, salt, and turmeric. Add the water and make a paste, then rub it all over the lamb chops and allow to marinate for 30 minutes at room temperature. Grind the almonds in a coffee grinder and mix them into the cream. Set aside.

Chop the onion finely. Grate the ginger and garlic. In a large heavy-bottomed saucepan over medium heat, warm the oil. Add the cumin. When it darkens (1 to 2 seconds), add the grated ginger and garlic. Cook for 1 minute, then add the chopped onion and saute until limp and translucent (about 5 minutes). Gently arrange the lamp chops over the onion and cook on all sides for 5 minutes. Mix in the tomatoes, cover, reduce the heat to low, and cook until the lamb is tender (about 40 minutes), stirring occasionally to prevent burning. Pour in the cream-almond mixture and sprinkle the fennel on top. Mix gently and heat through. Serve.

Yield: Serves 4 with other dishes.

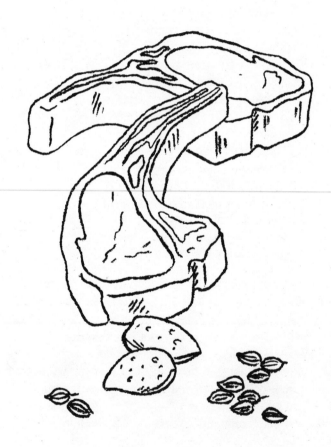

# Lamb in Coconut Milk

## *Meat Kari*

For people who associate Goan food only with *vindaloo*, this dish will come as a surprise. The lamb is cooked in creamy coconut milk with lots of fresh coriander—a good illustration of the incredible medley of cooking styles found in Goa.

1 pound boned and defatted lamb or beef
3 large cloves garlic
1 teaspoon coriander seeds
1/4 teaspoon fenugreek seeds
1/2 teaspoon ground turmeric
1 tablespoon fennel seeds
1/2-inch piece fresh ginger
2 green chillies (deseeded if desired)
1 cup fresh coriander leaves and tender upper
   stems
2 medium onions
3 tablespoons vegetable oil
1/2 teaspoon black mustard seeds
8 to 10 dried curry leaves
1 can (14 ounces) coconut milk
Salt, to taste
2 tablespoons distilled white vinegar

Cut the lamb into 1/2-inch cubes and set aside. Peel the garlic. In a small heavy-bottomed skillet over low heat, dry-roast together the garlic, coriander seeds, fenugreek, and turmeric until the garlic has a few brown specks and the coriander seeds smell roasted. Remove from the heat and let cool. Transfer the coriander seeds and fenugreek to the container of a coffee grinder along with the fennel; grind finely. Transfer the roasted garlic to the container of a blender or food processor along with the ginger, chillies, and fresh coriander; mince finely. Reserve the turmeric in the pan.

Chop the onions finely. In a large heavy-bottomed saucepan over medium heat, warm the oil. Add the mustard seeds and curry leaves. When the seeds splutter (1 to 2 seconds), add the chopped onions and saute until browned (about 10 minutes). Add the ground spices and the reserved turmeric from the pan. Cook for 1 minute. Add the lamb and cook until browned (about 5 minutes). Pour in the coconut milk and mix in the salt and vinegar. Bring to a boil, reduce the heat to low, cover, and cook for 30 minutes. Stir in the minced ginger mixture from the blender and cook covered for 15 minutes. Serve hot.

Yield: Serves 4 with other dishes.

# Lamb in Yogurt and Fennel
## *Yakhni*

This zesty stew from Kashmir is easy to prepare. The lamb in creamy yogurt-fennel sauce is perfect to eat with rice and a cucumber salad.

**1 pound boned and defatted lamb or beef**
**1 tablespoon fennel seeds**
**2 tablespoons vegetable oil**
**1-inch stick cinnamon**
**6 whole cloves**
**4 cardamom pods**
**1/2 teaspoon ground ginger**
**Salt, to taste**
**1/2 cup water**
**2/3 cup plain yogurt**
**1/2 teaspoon *garam masala***
**Fresh coriander leaves, for garnish**

Cut the lamb into 1-inch cubes. Grind the fennel seeds in a coffee grinder. In a large heavy-bottomed saucepan over medium heat, warm the oil. Add the cinnamon, cloves, and cardamom. When the spices puff up and darken (1 to 2 seconds), add the lamb and brown over medium heat for 5 minutes. Add the ground fennel seeds, ginger, and salt. Stir in the water, cover, increase the heat to high, and bring the contents of the pan to a boil. Reduce the heat to low and cook for 30 minutes. Beat the yogurt with a spoon until smooth, then gradually mix it into the lamb, stirring constantly. Cook covered until the lamb is tender (about 20 minutes). Mix in the *garam masala* and serve garnished with coriander leaves.

Yield: Serves 4 with other dishes.

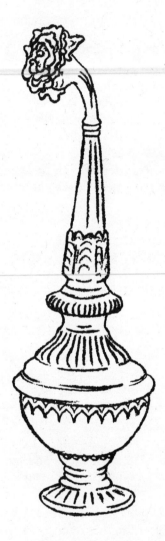

# Main Dishes: Chicken

You will note that in the dishes that call for chicken, I specify drumsticks or thighs rather than breasts. This is because dark meat takes longer to cook than white meat, which gives the flavors in the sauce time to blend thoroughly.

# Chicken with Herbs and Yogurt
## *Sindhi Murgh*

The chicken can be cooked directly in its marinade instead of pot-roasting it first. It can be baked in the oven too. If the sauce is very thin at the end of cooking, it should be boiled down. This dish can be served with Potatoes and Peas in Onion-Tomato Sauce and Pan-Broiled Wheat Bread.

**2 pounds chicken drumsticks or thighs, skinned**
**2 medium onions**
**1/2-inch piece fresh ginger**
**2 large cloves garlic**
**1 green chilli (optional)**
**1 cup fresh coriander leaves and tender upper**
  **stems**
**1/2 cup fresh mint leaves**
**4 tablespoons plain yogurt**
**1 teaspoon tamarind paste *or* 2 tablespoons lemon**
  **juice**
**1/2 teaspoon ground roasted cumin seeds**
**Salt, to taste**
**1/2 teaspoon ground turmeric**
**1/2 teaspoon *garam masala***
**3 tablespoons vegetable oil**

Pat the chicken dry, make deep gashes on the surface with a knife, and set aside. Chop the onions, ginger, garlic, and chilli (if used) coarsely. Place them in the container of a food processor or blender along with the coriander and mint. Blend to a smooth paste, adding 1 to 2 tablespoons water, if necessary. Transfer to a medium bowl and mix in the yogurt, tamarind (if using lemon juice add it at the end of cooking), cumin, salt, turmeric, and *garam masala*. Rub this paste over the chicken pieces and marinate for 2 to 3 hours in the refrigerator.

When ready to cook, scrape the marinade off the chicken and set the pieces aside on a plate. Reserve the marinade. In a large skillet, preferably nonstick, warm the oil over medium heat. Arrange the chicken pieces in a single layer and brown them lightly for 5 minutes on each side. Reduce the heat to low and mix in the reserved marinade. Cover and cook until the chicken is tender (about 25 minutes). Serve hot.

Yield: Serves 4 with other dishes.

# Chicken with Spinach
## *Saag Murgh*

2 pounds chicken drumsticks or thighs, skinned
20 ounces (2 packets) frozen chopped spinach
2 medium onions
3/4-inch piece fresh ginger
4 large cloves garlic
3 tablespoons vegetable oil
1 teaspoon cumin seeds
4 cardamom pods
6 whole cloves
1-inch stick cinnamon
1 teaspoon ground coriander seeds
1/2 teaspoon ground turmeric
Salt, to taste
1/4 teaspoon cayenne pepper
8 tablespoons plain yogurt
1/2 teaspoon *garam masala*

Pat the chicken dry and set aside. Thaw the spinach thoroughly and leave it in a colander to drain. Chop the onions finely. Grate the ginger and garlic. In a large saucepan over medium heat, warm the oil. Add the cumin, cardamom, cloves, and cinnamon. When the spices puff up and darken (in a second or so), add the grated ginger and garlic. Cook for 1 minute, then add the chopped onions and saute until lightly browned (about 8 minutes). Add the coriander, turmeric, salt, and cayenne. Saute for 1 minute, then gradually add the yogurt, stirring constantly. Cook for 2 minutes, then add the drained spinach. Mix well and cook for another 2 minutes. Add the chicken and stir to mix. Cover the pan, reduce the heat to low, and cook for 40 minutes, stirring occasionally. Uncover, increase the heat to medium-high, and boil off most of the liquid. Mix in the *garam masala* and serve. This tastes best the day after it is made.

Yield: Serves 4 with other dishes.

# Chicken with Mushrooms
## *Murghi Sabziwali*

2 pounds chicken drumsticks or thighs, skinned
1 medium onion
1/2-inch piece fresh ginger
4 cloves garlic
3 tablespoons vegetable oil
1/2 teaspoon cumin seeds
1 large green bell pepper, chopped into 1/2-inch pieces
3/4 cup coarsely chopped mushrooms
6 green onions, including green parts, chopped into 1-inch pieces
2 medium tomatoes, chopped coarsely, *or* 4 tablespoons plain yogurt, beaten lightly
Salt, to taste
1/4 teaspoon cayenne pepper
1/2 teaspoon ground turmeric
1/2 teaspoon ground coriander seeds
1/4 cup water
1/2 teaspoon *garam masala*

Pat the chicken dry and set aside. Chop the onion coarsely. Grate the ginger and garlic. In a large saucepan over medium heat, warm the oil. Add the cumin. When it darkens (1 to 2 seconds), add the grated ginger and garlic. Cook for 1 minute, then add the chopped onion and saute until lightly browned (7 to 8 minutes). Add the bell pepper and cook for 3 minutes. Add the mushrooms and cook for 3 more minutes. Add the green onions and cook for 3 minutes. Add the tomatoes. If using yogurt, add it gradually to the pan. Reduce the heat to low and cook for 5 to 7 minutes. Mix in the salt, cayenne, turmeric, and coriander. Add the chicken and the water. Cover and cook until tender (about 35 minutes). Mix in the *garam masala* and serve.

Yield: Serves 4 with other dishes.

# Chicken in Sour Cream and Nuts
## *Murgh Korma*

The Moghuls, famous for building the legendary Taj Mahal, were also connoisseurs of food. They left an unforgettable culinary legacy in India, especially in the North.

**2 pounds chicken drumsticks or thighs, skinned**
**12 almonds**
**2 medium onions**
**1/2-inch piece fresh ginger**
**4 cloves garlic**
**4 tablespoons vegetable oil**
**1 bay leaf**
**1/2 teaspoon cumin seeds**
**1/2 teaspoon ground coriander seeds**
**Salt, to taste**
**1/4 teaspoon cayenne pepper**
**1 tablespoon unsweetened desiccated coconut**
  **powder**
**4 tablespoons sour cream**
**1/2 teaspoon *garam masala***

Pat the chicken dry and set aside. Soak the almonds in warm water for 30 minutes; drain well. Chop the onions, ginger, and garlic coarsely. Place them along with the drained almonds in the container of a blender or food processor and mince finely. In a large saucepan over medium heat, warm the oil. Add the bay leaf and cumin. When the spices darken (1 to 2 seconds), add the minced onion mixture and saute until golden brown (about 12 minutes), stirring occasionally. Add the coriander, salt, cayenne, and coconut. Saute for 1 minute, then add the sour cream. Mix well. Add the chicken pieces, coating them well with the sauce. Cover, reduce the heat to low, and cook until the chicken is tender (about 40 minutes), stirring occasionally to prevent burning. Mix in the *garam masala* and serve.

Yield: Serves 4 with other dishes.

# Chicken with Fenugreek
## *Murgh Methi*

If you have fenugreek growing in your herb garden, this is the recipe to experiment with first. The fresh leaves are milder in flavor than the seeds and infinitely more aromatic. You can serve this dish with Potatoes in Creamy Yogurt Sauce and an Indian bread of your choice.

**2 medium onions**
**1/2-inch piece fresh ginger**
**4 cloves garlic**
**3 tablespoons vegetable oil**
**1/2 teaspoon cumin seeds**
**Salt, to taste**
**1/4 teaspoon cayenne pepper**
**1/2 teaspoon ground turmeric**
**2 cups fresh fenugreek leaves, chopped coarsely**
**1 pound chicken drumsticks or thighs, skinned**
**2 tablespoons lemon juice**

Slice the onions into thin half rounds. Grate the ginger and garlic. In a large saucepan over medium heat, warm the oil. Add the cumin. When it darkens (1 to 2 seconds), add the grated ginger and garlic. Cook for 1 minute, then add the sliced onions and saute until they brown lightly (about 8 minutes). Reduce the heat to low and add the salt, cayenne, turmeric, and fenugreek. Add the chicken pieces and coat them well with the onion mixture. Cover and cook for 30 minutes, stirring occasionally. Increase the heat to medium-low, uncover the pan, and cook until the chicken is tender and fairly dry and most of the liquid is boiled down (about 15 minutes). Sprinkle with lemon juice just before serving.

Yield: Serves 2 to 4 with other dishes.

# Chicken with Green Tomatoes
## *Hare Tamatar Wali Murghi*

Here is a good way to use up green tomatoes left after the frost. The tartness they add to the sauce is mellowed by the sour cream. This dish goes well with rice and a crunchy salad.

**2 pounds chicken drumsticks or thighs, skinned**
**1 medium onion**
**1/2-inch piece fresh ginger**
**3 tablespoons vegetable oil**
**1/2 teaspoon cumin seeds**
**1/2 teaspoon black mustard seeds**
**3 medium green tomatoes**
**5 tablespoons sour cream**
**Salt, to taste**
**1/4 teaspoon cayenne pepper**
**1/4 teaspoon ground turmeric**
**1/2 teaspoon ground fennel seeds**
**1/2 teaspoon ground coriander seeds**
**1/2 teaspoon *garam masala***

Pat the chicken dry with a paper towel; set aside. Chop the onion finely. Grate the ginger. In a large saucepan over medium heat, warm the oil. Add the cumin and mustard seeds. When the spices darken (1 to 2 seconds), add the grated ginger. Cook for 1 minute, then add the chopped onion and saute until golden brown (12 to 15 minutes). Puree the tomatoes in a food processor or blender. Mix in 3 tablespoons of the sour cream and blend again.

Add the salt, cayenne, turmeric, fennel, and coriander to the saucepan, cook for 1 minute, then add the tomato mixture. Cook for 2 minutes, then add the chicken. Cover, reduce the heat to low, and cook until the chicken is tender (about 40 minutes). Mix in the remaining 2 tablespoons of sour cream and the *garam masala*. Serve hot. If you want the sauce to be thicker, increase the heat to medium, uncover the pan, and boil down the sauce.

Yield: Serves 4 with other dishes.

# Chicken in Coconut Milk
## *Kozhi Molee*

A Kerala classic, this curry is redolent with black pepper. The region has always been a major producer of this spice, which is reflected in its cuisine. Fine strips of green bell pepper can be added just before serving.

**2 medium onions**
**1/2-inch piece fresh ginger**
**4 cloves garlic**
**3 tablespoons vegetable oil**
**Pinch crushed asafoetida (optional)**
**1/2 teaspoon black mustard seeds**
**1/2 teaspoon fenugreek seeds**
**10 dried curry leaves**
**1 tablespoon peppercorns, coarsely crushed**
**2 pounds chicken drumsticks or thighs, skinned**
**1 can (14 ounces) coconut milk**
**1/4 teaspoon ground turmeric**
**Salt, to taste**
**1 teaspoon tamarind paste dissolved in 2 tablespoons hot water *or* 2 teaspoons lemon juice and pinch sugar**

Finely chop the onions. Grate the ginger and garlic. In a large saucepan over medium heat, warm the oil. Add the asafoetida (if used), mustard seeds, fenugreek, and curry leaves. As soon as the seeds splutter, add the grated ginger and garlic. Cook for 1 minute, then add the chopped onions and saute until they are browned (12 to 15 minutes). Add the crushed peppercorns and saute 1 more minute. Add the chicken, coconut milk, turmeric, and salt. Mix well, cover, increase the heat to medium-high, and bring the contents of the pan to a boil. Reduce the heat to low and cook covered for 20 minutes. Uncover the pan and continue cooking over low heat for another 20 minutes, stirring occasionally. Mix in the dissolved tamarind paste. Serve hot.

Yield: Serves 4 with other dishes.

# Chicken in Coconut Milk and Peanuts

*Nariyal Ke Doodh Wala Murgh*

This original recipe came about when I was in a mood to experiment in the kitchen. Don't be intimidated by the long list of ingredients—the results will be worth it. I often serve this dish with rice and Peas with Ginger and Cumin.

2 medium onions
1-inch piece fresh ginger
4 large cloves garlic
2 tablespoons vegetable oil
2 teaspoons coriander seeds
1 teaspoon cumin seeds
2 whole cloves
2 cardamom pods
1/2 teaspoon peppercorns
1 dried red chilli
10 dried curry leaves
1/4 teaspoon fenugreek seeds
1/2 teaspoon black mustard seeds
1/2-inch stick cinnamon
1 teaspoon fennel seeds
1/2 teaspoon white poppy seeds
3/4 cup roasted, unsalted peanuts
Salt, to taste
1/2 teaspoon ground turmeric
1 can (14 ounces) coconut milk
2 pounds chicken drumsticks or thighs, skinned
4 tablespoons lemon juice

Chop the onions finely. Grate the ginger and garlic. In a large saucepan over medium heat, warm the oil. Add the grated ginger and garlic. Cook for 1 minute, then add the chopped onions and saute until lightly browned (about 8 minutes).

Meanwhile, in a small skillet over low heat, dry-roast the coriander, cumin, cloves, cardamom, peppercorns, chilli, curry leaves, fenugreek, mustard seeds, cinnamon, fennel, and poppy seeds. Cook until the spices darken (a few minutes), then let cool and grind. Grind the peanuts separately. Add them and the ground spices to the onion mixture, stir in the salt and turmeric, and add the coconut milk and chicken. Stir to mix, cover, reduce the heat to low, and cook until the chicken is tender (about 45 minutes). Mix in the lemon juice just before serving.

Yield: Serves 4 with other dishes.

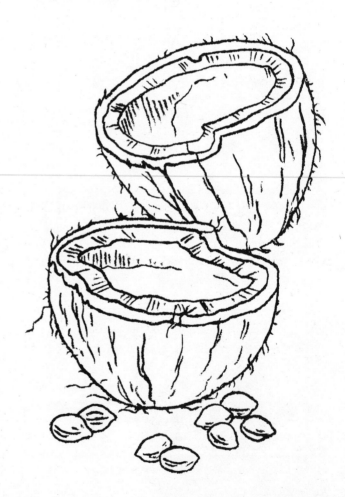

# Chicken with Coconut and Mint
## *Podhina Thenga Masala Kozhi*

Southern Indian cooking uses coconuts in a myriad of ways. Grated coconut is stir-fried with vegetables; coconut milk is used in making sauces; tender green coconut is added to desserts; and coconut water is served as a cooling drink. Spices such as coriander seeds, fenugreek seeds, mustard seeds, and curry leaves add their distinctive touch to produce the authentic South Indian flavor.

1 1/2 cups Thenga Chutney (coconut chutney)
1 cup fresh mint leaves
2 medium onions
3 tablespoons vegetable oil
1/2 teaspoon black mustard seeds
8 to 10 dried curry leaves
2 teaspoons coriander seeds
1 teaspoon cumin seeds
1/2 teaspoon fenugreek seeds
1/2-inch stick cinnamon
2 whole cloves
2 cardamom pods
1/2 teaspoon peppercorns
1 dried red chilli (optional)
2 pounds chicken drumsticks or thighs, skinned
Salt, to taste
1/2 teaspoon ground turmeric
Dash lemon juice

Place the coconut chutney in the container of a blender along with the mint and blend until smooth. Chop the onions finely. In a large saucepan over medium heat, warm the oil. Add the mustard seeds and curry leaves. As soon as the seeds splutter, add the chopped onions and saute until browned (10 to 12 minutes).

Meanwhile, in a small heavy-bottomed skillet over low heat, dry-roast the coriander, cumin, fenugreek, cinnamon, cloves, cardamom, peppercorns, and chilli (if used). Cook until the spices darken, then let cool, grind, and add to the onion mixture. Stir, then add the chutney-mint mixture, chicken, salt, and turmeric. Toss well to coat. Cover the pan, reduce the heat to low, and cook until the chicken is tender (about 40 minutes). Serve with lemon juice.

Yield: Serves 4 with other dishes.

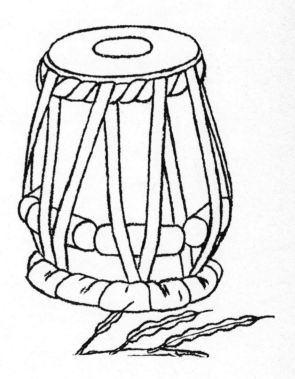

---

55

---

# Chicken in Tomato Puree

## *Murgh Lajawab*

This dish brings back memories of an autumn trip to Cambridge, England. After a day spent exploring cobbled streets, we revived ourselves with a chicken dinner at an Indian restaurant. This is my version of that satisfying dish. You can serve it with Pan-Broiled Leavened Bread or rice and accompany it with any vegetable of your choice.

**2 pounds chicken drumsticks or thighs, skinned**
**3/4 cup canned tomato puree**
**1/4 cup water**
**Salt, to taste**
**1/4 teaspoon cayenne pepper**
**1/2 teaspoon ground turmeric**
**4 cardamom pods**
**6 whole cloves**
**1/2-inch stick cinnamon**
**1/2 teaspoon peppercorns**
**1 bay leaf**
**2 medium onions**
**1 large green bell pepper**
**1/4-inch piece fresh ginger**
**4 cloves garlic**
**3 tablespoons vegetable oil**
**1/2 teaspoon cumin seeds**
**1/2 teaspoon ground coriander seeds**
**1 teaspoon ground fennel seeds**
**1/4 teaspoon *garam masala***
**1 tablespoon lemon juice**

In a large saucepan over high heat, place the chicken, tomato puree, the water, salt, cayenne, turmeric, cardamom, cloves, cinnamon, peppercorns, and bay leaf. Cover and bring to a boil, then reduce the heat to low and cook for 40 minutes. Remove the chicken pieces, let cool slightly, and take the meat off the bones. Reserve the meat and the puree mixture.

Mince together the onions, bell pepper, ginger, and garlic. In a large skillet over medium heat, warm the oil. Add the cumin. When it darkens (1 to 2 seconds), add the minced onion mixture and saute until the onion has brown specks (15 to 17 minutes). Add the coriander and fennel, stir for 1 minute, then add the reserved puree mixture. Mix well and add the chicken meat. Stir, then cook for 5 minutes more. Add the *garam masala* and lemon juice. Serve hot.

Note: The whole spices in this dish are not meant to be eaten.

Yield: Serves 4 with other dishes.

# Chicken with Yogurt and Mustard

## *Murghir Kari*

This is an unusual dish from Bengal, where they use a paste of pungent, ground mustard seeds on meat, fish or vegetable dishes. In this recipe the chicken is first roasted in the pot and then cooked in its marinade. The result is a wonderful, roasted mustardy flavor, which goes well with Cottage Cheese, Peas, and Nuts in Creamy Tomato Sauce and Pan-Broiled Leavened Bread..

**2 pounds chicken drumsticks or thighs, skinned**
**2 tablespoons black mustard seeds**
**1 tablespoon ground ginger**
**8 tablespoons plain yogurt**
**Salt, to taste**
**1/4 teaspoon cayenne pepper**
**2 medium onions**
**6 tablespoons vegetable oil**
**3/4-inch stick cinnamon**
**6 cardamom pods**
**6 whole cloves**
**1/4 cup water**

Pat the chicken dry and set aside. Place the mustard seeds in the container of a coffee grinder and grind finely. Transfer to a small bowl and add the ginger, yogurt, salt, and cayenne. Mix well. Rub this paste all over the chicken and marinate for 2 to 3 hours in the refrigerator.

Meanwhile, chop the onions finely. In a large, preferably non-stick skillet over medium-high heat, warm the oil. Add the cinnamon, cardamom, and cloves. As soon as the spices puff up and darken, add the chopped onions. Saute for about 5 minutes. Shake the marinade off the chicken or scrape it off with a spoon, reserving the marinade. Arrange the chicken pieces over the onions and sear on all sides until the chicken has brown spots (8 to 10 minutes). Reduce the heat to low. Mix the water into the reserved marinade and pour it over the chicken. Stir, cover, and cook until the chicken is tender (about 30 minutes). Serve hot.

Yield: Serves 4 with other dishes.

# Chicken with Yogurt and Cardamom

## *Murgh Elaichi*

Kashmiri cooking is noticeably different from that of other regions. It relies heavily on cardamom and fennel to spice its dishes, and it uses a lot of yogurt. The recipe given here is a good illustration of the cuisine and is an excellent accompaniment to Mushrooms with Peas and Pan-Broiled Wheat Bread.

**2 pounds chicken drumsticks or thighs, skinned**
**3/4-inch piece fresh ginger**
**2 cloves garlic**
**20 cardamom pods**
**5 tablespoons plain yogurt**
**3 teaspoons ground fennel seeds**
**Salt, to taste**
**1/4 teaspoon cayenne pepper**
**2 medium onions**
**3 tablespoons vegetable oil**
**4 whole cloves**
**1-inch stick cinnamon**
**1 bay leaf**
**1/2 teaspoon cumin seeds**

Pat the chicken dry with a paper towel, make a few cuts over the surface with a knife, and set aside. Grate the ginger and garlic. Remove the seeds from the cardamom pods and grind the seeds. Beat the yogurt with a spoon until smooth and add the grated ginger and garlic, fennel, half the ground cardamom, salt, and cayenne. Mix well. Rub this paste over the chicken pieces and marinate at room temperature for 1 hour or in the refrigerator overnight.

Chop the onions finely. In a large saucepan over medium heat, warm the oil. Add the cloves, cinnamon, bay leaf, and cumin. When the spices darken, add the chopped onions and saute until the onions are evenly browned (about 10 minutes). Reduce the heat to very low and add the chicken with its marinade. Cover and cook until the chicken is tender (35 to 40 minutes), stirring occasionally. Mix in the remaining ground cardamom and serve.

Yield: Serves 4 with other dishes.

# Chicken with Vinegar

## *Murgh Vindaloo*

Probably the best known Indian dish in the West, chicken vindaloo owes its popularity to the fact that many of the cooks who initially came to work abroad were from Goa. Like the rest of Goan food, chicken vindaloo can be fiery to the taste. The heat has been tempered somewhat in this recipe, but it can be further adjusted to suit personal taste. The vindaloo paste in which the chicken is marinated can be made up to a day ahead of time.

**2 pounds chicken drumsticks or thighs, skinned**
**2 medium onions**
**1/2-inch piece fresh ginger**
**4 large cloves garlic**
**5 tablespoons vegetable oil**
**5 tablespoons distilled white vinegar**
**1 teaspoon ground coriander seeds**
**1 teaspoon ground cumin seeds**
**1 teaspoon *garam masala***
**1/2 teaspoon freshly ground black pepper**
**Salt, to taste**
**1/2 teaspoon ground turmeric**
**1/2 teaspoon cayenne pepper**
**8 to 10 dried curry leaves**
**1/2 teaspoon black mustard seeds**
**1/4 cup water**
**1 large potato**
**Vegetable oil, for deep-frying**

Pat the chicken dry with a paper towel, make a few cuts over the surface with a knife, and set aside. Chop the onion, ginger, and garlic coarsely. In a large skillet over high heat, warm the 5 tablespoons oil. Add the chopped onions, ginger, and garlic, and saute until lightly browned (about 7 minutes). Remove from the heat and with a slotted spoon transfer the onion mixture to the container of a blender or food processor, leaving behind as much of the oil as possible. Add 3 tablespoons of the vinegar to the mixture and blend to a smooth paste.

Transfer the contents of the blender to a medium bowl and add the coriander, cumin, *garam masala*, black pepper, salt, turmeric, and cayenne. Mix well. Rub this paste well into the chicken pieces and let them marinate for 1 hour at room temperature.

Warm the oil remaining in the skillet over high heat and add the curry leaves and mustard. As soon as the mustard seeds splutter, add the chicken and its marinade. Sear for 5 minutes, turning the pieces so that they brown evenly. Reduce the heat to low, add the water, cover, and cook for 20 minutes.

Meanwhile, peel and cut the potato into 1-inch pieces. In a small skillet over medium-high heat, warm the oil for deep-frying. Add the potato and cook until golden. Drain, then add to the chicken along with the remaining 2 tablespoons vinegar. Cook covered for 10 minutes over low heat. Serve hot.

Yield: Serves 4 with other dishes.

# Chicken with Cashew Nuts

## *Malo Murghi*

The chicken, cooked in a spicy nut and cream sauce, is unlike other poultry and meat dishes in this book in taste and cooking style. It is good served with a lighter dish, such as Peas with Ginger and Cumin or Eggplant in Garlic-Herb Sauce.

**3/4 cup broken cashew nut pieces**
**2 tablespoons white sesame seeds**
**4 cardamom pods, seeds removed**
**4 whole cloves**
**1-inch stick cinnamon**
**1/2 teaspoon peppercorns**
**1/2-inch piece fresh ginger**
**2 cloves garlic**
**2 medium onions**
**3 tablespoons vegetable oil**
**1/2 teaspoon cumin seeds**
**1/4 teaspoon ground turmeric**
**Salt, to taste**
**1/4 teaspoon cayenne pepper**
**1/4 cup water**
**2 pounds chicken drumsticks or thighs, skinned**
**1 teaspoon *garam masala***
**1/2 cup whipping cream**
**Dash lemon juice**

In a large heavy-bottomed skillet over low heat, dry-roast the cashews, sesame seeds, cardamom seeds, cloves, cinnamon, and black peppercorns. Cook until they darken (a few minutes), then let cool and grind them. Grate the ginger and garlic. Chop the onions finely.

Warm the oil in a medium-size saucepan over medium heat. Add the cumin. When it darkens (1 to 2 seconds), add the grated ginger and garlic. Saute for 1 minute, then add the chopped onions and saute until well browned (10 to 12 minutes). Add the ground spice mixture, turmeric, salt, and cayenne. Stir in the water. Add the chicken, cover, reduce the heat to low, and cook until the chicken is tender (about 40 minutes), stirring occasionally. Add the *garam masala* and cream. Heat through and serve with lemon juice.

Yield: Serves 4 with other dishes.

# Chicken Curry

## *Bhuna Murgha*

This recipe combines the best of grilling and braising. The roasted aroma of the chicken and green bell peppers lifts this dish out of the ordinary. You could start it a day or two in advance if you are having a barbecue. Frozen skinned chicken may be grilled directly and kept refrigerated until added to the sauce.

2 pounds chicken drumsticks or thighs, skinned
2 medium green bell peppers
2 medium onions
1/2-inch piece fresh ginger
4 cloves garlic
3 tablespoons vegetable oil
1/2 teaspoon cumin seeds
2 medium tomatoes, chopped coarsely
1/2 teaspoon ground turmeric
1/2 teaspoon ground coriander seeds
1/2 teaspoon ground cumin seeds
1/2 teaspoon *garam masala*
1/4 teaspoon cayenne pepper
Salt, to taste
4 tablespoons plain yogurt
3/4 cup water

Lightly oil the chicken pieces and grill over a charcoal fire until lightly browned and cooked through. Set aside. Lightly oil the surface of the green bell peppers and grill, turning them over occasionally to ensure even cooking on all sides. Do not let them char. Let cool, then discard the seeds and stems and chop the peppers into 1-inch pieces. Set aside.

Chop the onions finely. Grate the ginger and garlic. In a large saucepan over medium heat, warm the oil. Add the cumin. When it darkens (1 to 2 seconds), add the grated ginger and garlic. Cook for 1 minute, then add the chopped onions and saute until browned (about 10 minutes). Add the tomatoes, turmeric, coriander, cumin, *garam masala*, cayenne, and salt. Cook until the tomatoes are soft (about 5 minutes). Reduce the heat to low, beat the yogurt lightly with a spoon, and add to the pan, stirring constantly. Cook for 2 minutes, then mix in the water. Add the grilled chicken and roasted peppers, cover, and cook for 15 minutes. Serve hot.

Yield: Serves 4 with other dishes.

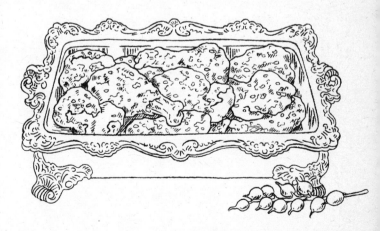

# Baked Chicken

## *Masalewali Dum Murghi*

In this dish, chicken is coated with a unique marinade and baked to perfection. It goes well with Spinach with Cottage Cheese and Pan-Broiled Leavened Bread. The marinade can be prepared up to a day ahead of time.

**2 pounds chicken drumsticks or thighs, skinned**
**3 tablespoons vegetable oil**
**1 teaspoon cumin seeds**
**1 teaspoon coriander seeds**
**1/2 teaspoon fenugreek seeds**
**1/2 teaspoon peppercorns**
**1-inch stick cinnamon**
**6 cardamom pods**
**6 whole cloves**
**1 dried red chilli (optional)**
**2 tablespoons unsweetened dried coconut flakes**
**1 tablespoon white poppy seeds**
**1-inch piece fresh ginger**
**4 cloves garlic**
**2 medium onions**
**2 medium tomatoes**
**5 tablespoons plain yogurt**
**Salt, to taste**

Make deep cuts over the surface of the chicken with a knife; set aside. In a large skillet over medium heat, warm the oil. Add the cumin, coriander, fenugreek, peppercorns, cinnamon, cardamom, cloves, and red chilli (if used). The spices will puff up and darken in a second. Quickly add the coconut and poppy seeds and cook until they brown lightly (about 2 more seconds). With a slotted spoon transfer the fried spices to the container of a blender, leaving behind as much oil as possible.

Grate the ginger and garlic. Chop the onions coarsely. To the remaining oil in the skillet, add the grated ginger and garlic. Cook for 1 minute over medium heat, then add the chopped onions and saute until browned (9 to 10 minutes). Transfer the onions to the blender container, add the tomatoes, and blend to a smooth paste. Mix in the yogurt and salt. Rub this marinade over the chicken pieces and place them in a baking dish. Seal the dish tightly with aluminum foil and let it stand for 1 hour. Bake in a preheated oven at 400°F for 45 minutes.

Yield: Serves 4 with other dishes.

# Main Dishes: Seafood

# Shrimp in Sour Cream Sauce
## *Jhinga Malaidaar*

This dish, a favorite of our family, tastes good over a mound of steaming rice with a cool crunchy salad on the side. If you find this dish too hot, reduce the amount of ground pepper. Serve this shrimp with a mild vegetable dish, such as Potatoes in Coriander-Yogurt Sauce.

**1 pound shrimp, shelled and deveined**
**2 cloves garlic**
**1 medium onion**
**2 tablespoons vegetable oil**
**1 teaspoon cumin seeds**
**1 teaspoon ground coriander seeds**
**1 teaspoon coarsely ground pepper**
**Salt, to taste**
**4 tablespoons sour cream**
**1/4 cup water**
**Dash fresh lemon juice (optional)**
**Chopped fresh coriander leaves (optional)**

Wash the shrimp and pat dry with a paper towel; set aside. Chop the garlic and onion finely. In a large skillet over medium heat, warm the oil. Add the cumin. When it darkens (1 to 2 seconds), add the chopped garlic and onion and saute until golden brown (about 12 minutes). Reduce the heat to low and add the ground coriander seeds, pepper, and salt. Add the sour cream and the water. Mix in the shrimp, cover, and cook until the shrimp feel firm to the touch (about 8 minutes). Serve with lemon juice and fresh coriander leaves, if desired.

Yield: Serves 4 with other dishes.

# Shrimp in Onion-Yogurt Sauce
## *Jhinga Dahiwala*

This wonderfully simple, easy-to-master shrimp dish tastes delicious with rice. If you are cooking Indian-style shrimp for the first time, this is the no-fail recipe to impress the family.

**1 pound shrimp, shelled and deveined**
**1/2-inch piece fresh ginger**
**2 cloves garlic**
**2 medium onions**
**3 tablespoons vegetable oil**
**1 teaspoon cumin seeds**
**1 teaspoon ground coriander seeds**
**Salt, to taste**
**1/4 teaspoon cayenne pepper**
**1/2 teaspoon ground turmeric**
**5 tablespoons plain yogurt**
**1/4 cup water**
**3/4 teaspoon *garam masala***
**Dash lemon juice (optional)**
**Chopped fresh coriander leaves (optional)**

Wash the shrimp and pat dry with a paper towel; set aside. Grate the ginger and garlic. Chop the onions finely. In a large skillet over medium heat, warm the oil. Add the cumin. When it darkens (1 to 2 seconds), add the grated ginger and garlic. Cook for 1 minute, then add the chopped onions and saute until lightly browned (about 12 minutes). Reduce the heat to low and add the ground coriander seeds, salt, cayenne, and turmeric. Beat the yogurt with a spoon and add it to the pan, stirring constantly. Cook for about 10 minutes, stirring once or twice. Add the shrimp and the water. Mix, cover, and cook until the shrimp feel firm to the touch (about 8 minutes). Mix in the *garam masala* and serve with lemon juice and fresh coriander leaves, if desired.

Yield: Serves 4 with other dishes.

# Shrimp with Tomatoes

*Jhinga Tamatari*

This simple dish is lifted out of the ordinary by the addition of fresh tomatoes and coriander, which are folded in at the last minute. It's a good brunch dish that also tastes good cold, so you can take it along on picnics.

1 pound shrimp, shelled and deveined
1/2-inch piece fresh ginger
2 cloves garlic
1 medium onion
2 tablespoons vegetable oil
1 teaspoon cumin seeds
1/2 teaspoon ground coriander seeds
Salt, to taste
1/2 teaspoon ground turmeric
1/4 teaspoon cayenne pepper
1/2 teaspoon *garam masala*
1 large tomato, chopped finely
2 tablespoons chopped fresh coriander leaves
1 tablespoon lemon juice

Wash the shrimp and pat dry with a paper towel; set aside. Grate the ginger and garlic. Chop the onion finely. In a large skillet over medium heat, warm the oil. Add the cumin. When it darkens (1 to 2 seconds), add the grated ginger and garlic. Cook for 1 minute, then add the chopped onion and saute until lightly browned (about 10 minutes). Reduce the heat to low, add the ground coriander seeds, salt, turmeric, and cayenne; then add the shrimp, cover, and cook until the shrimp feel firm to the touch (about 8 minutes). Remove from the heat and mix in the *garam masala*. Add the tomato, fresh coriander leaves, and lemon juice. Serve immediately.

Yield: Serves 4 with other dishes.

# Shrimp in Tomato Sauce

*Jhinga Masala Tamatarwala*

Serve these shrimp with a dry vegetable dish, such as Green Bell Peppers Stuffed with Potatoes or Potatoes in Creamy Yogurt Sauce and an Indian bread of your choice. If you wish to serve this dish with rice, add 1/4 cup water to the sauce.

1 pound shrimp, shelled and deveined
1/2-inch piece fresh ginger
2 cloves garlic
2 medium onions
2 tablespoons vegetable oil
1 teaspoon cumin seeds
1/2 teaspoon fennel seeds
3 medium tomatoes, chopped finely
1 teaspoon ground coriander seeds
1/2 teaspoon ground turmeric
Salt, to taste
1/4 teaspoon cayenne pepper
3/4 teaspoon *garam masala*

Wash the shrimp and pat dry with a paper towel; set aside. Grate the ginger and garlic. Chop the onions finely. In a large skillet over medium heat, warm the oil. Add the cumin and fennel. When the spices darken (1 to 2 seconds), add the chopped ginger and garlic. Cook for 1 minute, then add the chopped onions and saute until lightly browned (about 12 minutes). Add the tomatoes, coriander, turmeric, salt, and cayenne. Cook until the tomatoes are soft (about 10 minutes), mashing them well with the back of a spoon. Reduce the heat to low and add the shrimp. Mix, cover, and cook until the shrimp feel firm to the touch (about 8 minutes). Add the *garam masala* and serve.

Yield: Serves 4 with other dishes.

# Shrimp with Fenugreek
## *Masala Jhinga Methiwala*

Ask your Indian grocer for *kasoori methi*. They are dried fenugreek leaves named for Qasur, Pakistan, where the world's most flavorful fenugreek is grown.

1 1/2 pounds shrimp, shelled and deveined
2 medium tomatoes
1/2-inch piece fresh ginger
4 large cloves garlic
2 medium onions
1 teaspoon cumin seeds
6 tablespoons vegetable oil
2 teaspoons ground coriander seeds
Salt, to taste
1/4 to 1/2 teaspoon cayenne pepper
1/2 teaspoon ground turmeric
3 heaping tablespoons dried fenugreek leaves
2 tablespoons whipping cream

Wash the shrimp and pat completely dry with a paper towel. Chop the tomatoes coarsely and puree in the blender. Set the shrimp and tomatoes aside. In a food processor or blender, mince the ginger, garlic, onions, and 1/2 teaspoon of the cumin. In a large skillet over medium heat, warm the oil. Add the remaining 1/2 teaspoon cumin. When it darkens (1 to 2 seconds), add the minced onion mixture and saute until browned (about 10 minutes). Add the coriander, salt, cayenne, and turmeric and saute for 2 more minutes. Add the tomatoes and fenugreek. Cook for 5 minutes. Add the shrimp and saute for 6 to 7 minutes, stirring frequently. Remove from the heat, then mix in the whipping cream. Let the mixture stand in the covered pan for 7 to 10 minutes for the flavors to mingle.

Yield: Serves 4 with other dishes.

# Batter-Fried Shrimp
## *Tala Masalewala Jhinga*

1 pound shrimp, shelled and deveined
1/4-inch piece fresh ginger
1 clove garlic
1 small onion
1/4 cup fresh coriander leaves
1 tablespoon lemon juice
1 egg
Salt, to taste
1/2 teaspoon ground turmeric
1/4 teaspoon cayenne pepper
1/2 teaspoon ground coriander seeds
1/4 teaspoon ground cumin seeds
1/2 teaspoon *kalonji* (onion seeds) or cumin seeds
1/4 cup bread crumbs
1/4 cup chickpea flour
Vegetable oil, for deep-frying

Wash the shrimp and pat dry with a paper towel. Place the ginger, garlic, onion, fresh coriander leaves, and lemon juice in the container of a blender and blend to a fine paste. Transfer to a bowl and mix in the egg, salt, turmeric, cayenne, ground coriander, cumin, and onion seeds. Toss in the shrimp and marinate in this mixture for 15 minutes or longer in the refrigerator. Meanwhile, mix the bread crumbs and flour and keep in a bowl near the stove. In a large skillet over medium-high heat, warm the oil for deep-frying. Remove the shrimp from the marinade, then roll each shrimp in the bread crumb-flour mixture and slide gently into the hot oil. Add as many shrimp as will fit in a single layer. Cook until the shrimp are golden, turning occasionally. Repeat with remaining shrimp. Drain on paper towels and serve.

Yield: Serves 4 with other dishes.

# Fish in Tamarind Sauce

## *Machali Imliwali*

This simple, quickly prepared dish stands out from the ordinary because of the subtle tartness of the tamarind and the heat of the ground pepper. If this dish is too hot for your taste, you can reduce the amount of pepper used. Serve this fish with a dry potato dish, such as Potatoes with Scallions and any bread of your choice.

**1 pound cod fillets**
**1 teaspoon tamarind paste**
**4 tablespoons hot water**
**1/2-inch piece fresh ginger**
**2 large cloves garlic**
**Salt, to taste**
**1/2 teaspoon ground coriander seeds**
**1/2 teaspoon ground cumin seeds**
**1/2 teaspoon ground turmeric**
**1 teaspoon coarsely ground pepper**
**2 tablespoons vegetable oil, for shallow-frying**
**Dash lemon juice**

Wash the fillets and dry them well with a paper towel. Dissolve the tamarind in the hot water. Grate the ginger and garlic, and add to the tamarind water, along with the salt, coriander, cumin, turmeric, and pepper. Rub this paste all over the fish fillets. Cover and marinate at room temperature for 15 minutes, or longer in the refrigerator.

You can either shallow-fry the fillets in a skillet or broil them in the oven. To shallow-fry, in a nonstick skillet over medium heat, warm the oil. Add the fish along with its marinade. Cook until the fish is tender and flaky (about 5 minutes on each side). To broil, place the fish and all its marinade in a greased broiler pan about 7 inches away from the heat source. Cook until the fish is tender and flaky (about 5 minutes on each side). Serve with lemon juice.

Yield: Serves 4 with other dishes.

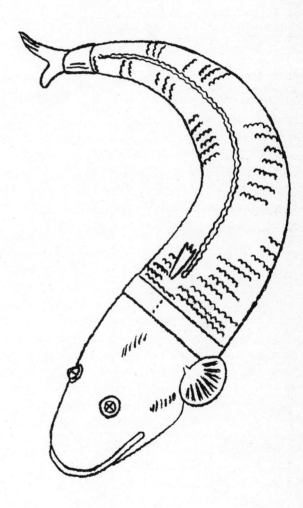

# Fish Curry
## *Machali Kari*

Using this basic curry recipe, you can substitute chicken, meat, vegetables, or boiled eggs for the fish. Just omit the initial marinating and frying and increase the cooking times.

**1 1/2 pounds haddock fillets**
**3/4 teaspoon ground turmeric**
**Salt, to taste**
**1/4 teaspoon cayenne pepper**
**2 teaspoons plus 1 cup water**
**1/2-inch piece fresh ginger**
**4 cloves garlic**
**2 medium onions**
**1/2 teaspoon cumin seeds**
**1/2 teaspoon ground coriander seeds**
**1 large tomato, chopped finely**
**4 tablespoons plain yogurt**

Cut the fillets into 2-inch chunks. Make a paste of the turmeric, salt, cayenne, and the 2 teaspoons water; smear it over the fish pieces. Allow to marinate for 15 minutes.

Mince the ginger, garlic, and onions; set aside. In a large skillet over high heat, warm the oil. Add the fish pieces and cook for 1 minute on each side. Remove carefully with a slotted spoon and set aside. Add the cumin to the oil. When the cumin seeds darken (1 to 2 seconds), add the minced onion mixture. Reduce the heat to medium and saute until the onions are browned (about 10 minutes). Add the coriander and tomato. Cook until soft (about 5 minutes). Beat the yogurt with a spoon and add it to the pan, stirring constantly. Cook for another 5 minutes, then add the 1 cup water and bring to a boil. Reduce the heat to low and gently slide in the pieces of fish. Cook for 5 to 7 minutes. Serve hot.

Yield: Serves 4 with other dishes.

# Fish in Herb Sauce
## *Hari Machali*

Fragrant with fresh coriander, this is a wonderful summertime dish. If you grill it on an outdoor barbecue, the neighbors may drop by for a taste.

**1 pound fish fillets (cod or similar variety)**
**1 cup fresh coriander leaves and tender upper**
  **stems**
**1 small onion**
**1/2-inch piece fresh ginger**
**2 tablespoons plain yogurt**
**1/2 teaspoon ground cumin seeds**
**1 teaspoon ground coriander seeds**
**1/2 teaspoon freshly ground pepper**
**Salt, to taste**
**2 tablespoons vegetable oil**
**Dash lemon juice**

Wash the fillets and dry them thoroughly with a paper towel. Place the fresh coriander leaves, onion, and ginger in the container of a blender and blend to a fine paste. Transfer to a bowl and add the yogurt, cumin, ground coriander seeds, pepper, and salt. Rub this paste all over the fish fillets, cover, and marinate at room temperature for 15 minutes, or longer in the refrigerator.

You can either shallow-fry the fillets in a skillet or broil them in the oven. To shallow-fry, in a nonstick skillet over medium heat, warm the oil. Add the fish with all its marinade. Cook until the fish is tender and flaky (5 to 7 minutes on each side). To broil, place the fish with all its marinade in a greased broiler pan about 5 to 7 inches away from the heat source. Cook until the fish is tender and flaky (5 to 7 minutes on each side). Serve with lemon juice.

Yield: Serves 4 with other dishes.

# Legumes

The dried legumes used in this book include dried beans, split peas, chickpeas, and lentils (or *dals* as they are known in India). My father-in-law, who made the best dal I have ever tasted, was in charge of the all-important *baghar*—the spiced garlicky butter that is poured on the dal just before serving. Early in the evening the dal would be cooked with onions, ginger, and turmeric, then set aside. When the family was ready to eat dinner, my father-in-law would go into the kitchen, prepare the baghar, and bring out the steaming pot of dal to the accompaniment of enthusiastic and hungry squeals from the children.

Legumes are an essential part of the Indian meal—they are especially indispensable to vegetarians, since they are often the principal source of protein. There are many legumes to choose from, ranging from the whole and unhulled variety to the split and hulled kind.

Each region has its own special way of cooking legumes. In the northern state of Uttar Pradesh, where I come from, we cook them with sliced onions, ginger, salt, and turmeric, then pour on melted butter or ghee in which garlic, dried red chillies, cumin, and asafoetida have been fried. In the state of Punjab, cooked chickpeas or kidney beans are added to a spicy sauce of onions, garlic, and tomatoes. In the South, a spicy, hot dal called *sambhar* is cooked with different vegetables. In Bengal, legumes are often cooked with meats.

Legumes are also served at festivals and special occasions. During the South Indian festival of Pongal, a sugary-sweet creation of lentils and coconut is offered to the gods; during North Indian weddings, a halva made from split, hulled mung beans browned in lots of butter and cooked with sugar is often served. Just as Americans reach for grandmother's chicken soup when they are sick, we comfort ourselves with *khichadi*, a nourishing, soothing dish made from rice and lentils. It will come as no surprise, then, to know that legumes are among the first foods fed to babies, and that most children love them.

Legumes can also be made into salads, appetizers, snacks, dumplings, and pancakes. My mother even makes pickles of chickpeas combined with sour mangoes and spices. An unusual salad I once had in the southern city of Bangalore consisted of presoaked uncooked lentils tossed with chopped cucumbers and lemon juice. You can see that the variety and versatility of legumes are endless.

This chapter gives you just a glimpse of how legumes can be used in different ways. Give your imagination free rein and create your own dishes. A word of advice before you start: When ordering from an Indian grocery store, use the Indian name of the legume as well as the English one to make sure that you receive the right ingredient. I have provided Indian names for each legume used in this book. Also, be sure to pick out the stones and other foreign matter often found in legumes. If you have a pressure cooker, do use it for faster results. Soak dried legumes for at least 30 minutes before cooking, and cook until tender but not mushy. Although asafoetida is listed as optional in these recipes, it is widely used with legumes because it makes them more digestible.

# Spicy Lentils
## *Masoor Masala*

For the majority of Indians who are vegetarian, dals are the main source of protein. There is an incredible variety of dals to choose from, and their versatility can be seen in the many preparations made from them. This basic recipe can be used to cook any kind of dal. You can also make soup out of these *dals* by adding water.

1 cup *sabut masoor* (whole brown lentils)
4 cups water
Salt, to taste
1/2 teaspoon ground turmeric
2 medium onions
2 cloves garlic
2 tablespoons vegetable oil
Tiny pinch crushed asafoetida (optional)
1 teaspoon cumin seeds
1 teaspoon ground coriander seeds
1/4 teaspoon cayenne pepper
1 large tomato, chopped coarsely
Dash lemon juice

Wash the lentils, place them and the water in a large, heavy-bottomed saucepan, and let soak for 1 hour. Add the salt and turmeric, and cook covered over low heat until tender (about 30 minutes).

Meanwhile, chop the onions and garlic finely. In a small heavy-bottomed skillet over medium heat, warm the oil. Add the asafoetida (if used) and cumin. When the spices darken (1 to 2 seconds), add the chopped onions and garlic and cook until browned (8 to 10 minutes). Add the coriander, cayenne, and tomato; cook until the tomato is soft (about 5 minutes).

When the lentils are cooked, add the onion-tomato mixture, stir, and cook for another 5 minutes. Serve with lemon juice.

Yield: Serves 4 with other dishes.

# Lentils with Cinnamon and Mixed Vegetables
## *Masoor Dal Sabziwali*

This wholesome dish combining lentils and vegetables is a meal by itself when accompanied by rice. By thinning it further with chicken stock, you can also serve it as a hearty soup.

3/4 cup *sabut masoor* (whole brown lentils)
3 cups water
Salt, to taste
1/2 teaspoon ground turmeric
2 medium onions
1/2-inch piece fresh ginger
3 cloves garlic
3 tablespoons vegetable oil
Pinch crushed asafoetida (optional)
1-inch stick cinnamon
1/2 teaspoon cumin seeds
1 bay leaf
1 cup chopped mixed frozen vegetables, thawed
3 medium tomatoes, chopped coarsely

Wash the lentils, place them and the water in a large heavy-bottomed saucepan, and let soak for 1 hour. Add the salt and turmeric, bring to a boil over high heat, then reduce the heat to low and cook covered until tender (about 30 minutes).

Meanwhile, chop the onions finely and grate the ginger and garlic. In a large heavy-bottomed skillet over medium heat, warm the oil. Add the asafoetida (if used), cinnamon, cumin, and bay leaf. When the spices darken (1 to 2 seconds), add the grated ginger and garlic. Cook for 1 minute, then add the chopped onions and cook for 7 to 8 minutes. Add the thawed vegetables and cook until almost tender (8 to 10 minutes). Add the tomatoes and cook for 5 minutes. Stir this mixture into the lentils, cover, and cook over low heat for 5 minutes.

Yield: Serves 4 with other dishes.

# Lentils with Fenugreek
### Dal Methiwali

The cuisine of Uttar Pradesh is characterized by its simplicity. Elaborate cooking techniques are rarely employed. The emphasis is on the main ingredient in the dish, with spices used cleverly to bring out its flavor.

1/3 cup *chana dal* (yellow split peas)
1/3 cup *dhuli urad dal* (split and hulled black gram beans)
2 cups water
1 small onion
1/4-inch piece fresh ginger
Salt, to taste
1/2 teaspoon ground turmeric
2 tablespoons dried fenugreek leaves *or*
   1/2 teaspoon fenugreek seeds
2 cloves garlic
1 tablespoon ghee or butter
1/2 teaspoon cumin seeds
Pinch crushed asafoetida (optional)
1/4 teaspoon cayenne pepper
1/4 teaspoon ground coriander seeds
1/4 teaspoon *garam masala*
1 tablespoon lemon juice

Wash the split peas and gram beans, place them and the water in a large heavy-bottomed saucepan, and let soak for 30 minutes. Chop the onion and ginger finely. Add to the soaked lentils along with the salt, turmeric, and fenugreek leaves. (If using the seeds add them later.) Bring to a boil over high heat, cover, reduce the heat to very low, and cook for 45 minutes. Remove from the heat.

Chop the garlic finely. In a small pan or butter warmer over medium heat, warm the ghee. Add the cumin and asafoetida (if used). If using fenugreek seeds add them now. When the spices darken (1 to 2 seconds), add the chopped garlic and cook until lightly browned. Remove from the heat and quickly add the cayenne and coriander. Stir for 1 second, then pour this mixture, including the ghee, into the lentil mixture. Cover and let stand for 5 minutes. Mix in the *garam masala* and lemon juice, and serve.

Yield: Serves 4 with other dishes.

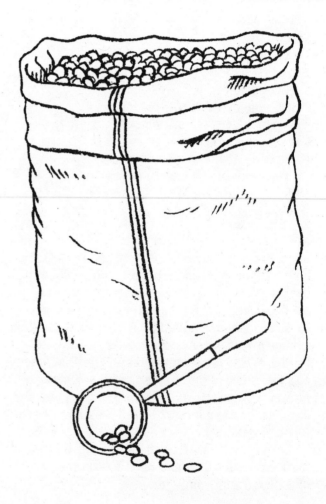

# Lentils with Sour Cream
## *Urad Malai*

Originally from Punjab, this dish has been made popular all over northern India by *dhabas*, the roadside cafes.

1 cup *sabut urad* (whole black gram beans)
3 1/2 cups water
Salt, to taste
1/2 cup cooked kidney beans
3 tablespoons sour cream, beaten with a spoon
1/4-inch piece fresh ginger
2 cloves garlic
1 tablespoon ghee or butter
Pinch crushed asafoetida (optional)
1 teaspoon cumin seeds
5 tablespoons canned crushed tomatoes
1 teaspoon *garam masala*
1/4 teaspoon cayenne pepper

Wash the gram beans well, place them and 2 cups of the water in a large heavy-bottomed saucepan, and let soak for at least 4 hours or overnight. Add the remaining 1 1/2 cups water and salt. Cover and bring to a boil over high heat. Reduce the heat to low and cook until the beans are soft and mushy (about 45 minutes), stirring occasionally. Remove from the heat and mash lightly with the back of a spoon. Add the cooked kidney beans and sour cream.

Grate the ginger and garlic. In a small heavy-bottomed skillet over medium heat, warm the ghee. Add the asafoetida (if used) and cumin. When the spices darken (1 to 2 seconds), add the grated ginger and garlic. Cook for 2 minutes, then add the tomatoes. Decrease the heat to medium-low and cook 2 to 3 minutes. Stir in the *garam masala* and cayenne, pour this mixture into the bean mixture, and cook over medium-low heat for 5 minutes. Serve hot.

Yield: Serves 4 with other dishes.

# Lentils with Mangoes
## *Dal Aamwali*

1 cup *tur dal* (yellow lentils)
4 cups water
1/2-inch piece fresh ginger
1 small onion
1/2 raw green mango (1/2 pound) *or*
  2 tablespoons lemon juice
Salt, to taste
1/2 teaspoon ground turmeric
2 large cloves garlic
1 tablespoon ghee or butter
Pinch crushed asafoetida (optional)
1/2 teaspoon cumin seeds
1/2 teaspoon ground coriander seeds
1/4 teaspoon cayenne pepper
1/2 teaspoon *garam masala*

Wash the lentils well, place them and the water in a large heavy-bottomed saucepan, and let soak for 1 hour or more. Meanwhile, finely chop the ginger and onion. Peel the mango and dice it into 1/2-inch cubes. (If using lemon juice, add it just before serving.) Add the chopped ginger and onion, diced mango, salt, and turmeric to the lentils, cover, and bring to a boil over high heat. Reduce the heat to low and cook until the lentils are tender (25 to 30 minutes). Set aside.

Chop the garlic finely. In a small pan over a high heat, warm the ghee. Add the chopped garlic and cook for 2 minutes. Add the asafoetida (if used) and cumin. As soon as the seeds splutter, remove from the heat and immediately add the coriander and cayenne. Pour this mixture, including the ghee, into the lentil mixture. Stir in the *garam masala* and serve.

Yield: Serves 4 with other dishes.

# Lentils with Spinach

## *Kire Sambhar*

*good*

Ready-made sambhar powder is available in all Indian grocery stores and can be used in place of all the roasted spices in this recipe. If you want to add more vegetables to this dish, use chopped green bell peppers, potatoes, okra, eggplant, or green beans in place of, or in addition to, the spinach.

3/4 cup *tur dal* (yellow lentils)
4 cups water
Salt, to taste
1/2 teaspoon ground turmeric
5 ounces frozen chopped spinach, thawed
2 1 medium tomato, chopped
1 1/2 teaspoons coriander seeds
1 teaspoon cumin seeds
1/2 teaspoon fenugreek seeds
1/4 1/2 teaspoon peppercorns
Pinch crushed asafoetida (optional)
2 whole cloves
1/2 1 teaspoon black mustard seeds
1 dried red chilli (optional)
18 dried curry leaves
1/2 1 medium onion
1/2-inch piece fresh ginger
2 cloves garlic
2 tablespoons vegetable oil
1/4 3/4 teaspoon tamarind paste
2 to 3 tablespoons grated fresh coconut
    (optional)

Wash the lentils well, place them and the water in a large heavy-bottomed saucepan, and let soak for 1 hour or more. Add the salt, turmeric, spinach, and tomato. Cover, bring to a boil over high heat, reduce the heat to low, and cook until the lentils are tender (about 45 minutes).

Meanwhile, in a small heavy-bottomed skillet over low heat, dry-roast together the coriander, cumin, fenugreek, peppercorns, asafoetida (if used), cloves, 1/2 teaspoon of the mustard seeds, chilli (if used), and 8 to 10 curry leaves. Cook until the spices darken (a few minutes). Let cool, then grind finely. Set aside.

Peel and slice the onion into thin half rounds. Grate the ginger and garlic. Increase the heat to medium under the skillet and warm the oil. Add the remaining 1/2 teaspoon mustard seeds and 8 curry leaves. When the seeds splutter, add the ginger and garlic. Cook for 1 minute, then add the onion and cook until lightly browned (about 8 minutes).

To the cooked lentils add the sauteed onion, roasted spices, tamarind paste, and coconut (if used). Mix well and continue cooking for another 5 minutes. Serve hot.

Yield: Serves 4 with other dishes.

# Mung Beans with Cottage Cheese

## *Moong Dal Paneerwali*

This unusual dish is cooked until dry, then tossed with grated coconut and cottage cheese. It is best served with an Indian bread of your choice and a wet vegetable dish, such as Zucchini Dumplings in Onion-Tomato Sauce. It can also be mashed lightly with cooked potatoes and formed into croquettes, or used as a stuffing for tomatoes.

**1 cup *sabut moong* (whole mung beans)**
**3 cups water**
**1/2-inch piece fresh ginger**
**3 tablespoons vegetable oil**
**Pinch crushed asafoetida (optional)**
**1/2 teaspoon cumin seeds**
**1/2-inch stick cinnamon**
**Salt, to taste**
**1/4 teaspoon cayenne pepper**
**1/2 teaspoon ground turmeric**
**1 medium onion**
**1 cup homemade cottage cheese, crumbled**
**3/4 cup grated fresh coconut**
**3/4 teaspoon *garam masala***
**2 tablespoons lemon juice**

Wash the mung beans and let soak in the 3 cups water for 3 hours. Meanwhile, grate the ginger. In a large heavy-bottomed saucepan over medium heat, warm 1 tablespoon of the oil. Add the asafoetida (if used), cumin, and cinnamon. When the spices darken (1 to 2 seconds), add the grated ginger and cook for 1 minute. Add the salt, cayenne, turmeric, and mung beans with 1 cup of their soaking water. Stir to mix, cover, increase the heat to high, and bring to a boil. Reduce the heat to medium and cook for 20 minutes without uncovering the pan. If any water is left at the end of the cooking time, uncover the pan and boil it off.

Slice the onion into thin half rounds. In a small skillet over medium heat, warm the remaining 2 tablespoons of oil. Add the sliced onion and cook until well browned (about 12 minutes). Remove with a slotted spoon and spread on a paper towel. In a small bowl combine 3/4 cup of the cottage cheese and the coconut. Stir in the *garam masala* and lemon juice, then add this mixture to the mung beans, stirring it in gently. Transfer to a serving dish and sprinkle the remaining 1/4 cup cottage cheese over the top. Spread the cooked onions evenly over all and serve.

Yield: Serves 4 with other dishes.

# Mung Beans with Vinegar-Soaked Spices

## *Moong Sirkewali*

Soaking the spices in vinegar draws out an entirely new flavor from them. You may serve this dish with Tomatoes with Cottage Cheese and Pan-Broiled Wheat Bread.

**1 cup *sabut moong* (whole mung beans)**
**3 cups water**
**3 tablespoons distilled white vinegar**
**2 cloves garlic**
**1 green chilli (optional)**
**1/2-inch piece fresh ginger**
**1/2 teaspoon peppercorns**
**1/2-inch stick cinnamon**
**5 cloves**
**3 cardamom pods**
**1 medium onion**
**2 tablespoons vegetable oil**
**1/2 teaspoon cumin seeds**
**1 bay leaf**
**1/2 teaspoon ground turmeric**
**Salt, to taste**

Wash the mung beans, place them and 2 cups of the water in a large heavy-bottomed saucepan, and let soak for 2 hours or more. Meanwhile, pour the vinegar into a small bowl and add the whole garlic, chilli (if used), ginger, peppercorns, cinnamon, cloves, and cardamom. Let soak for 30 minutes. Slice the onion into thin half rounds. In a small heavy-bottomed skillet over medium heat, warm the oil. Add the cumin and bay leaf. When the spices darken (1 to 2 seconds), add the sliced onion. Saute for 6 to 7 minutes, remove from the heat, and set aside.

To the mung beans add the turmeric, salt, and the remaining 1 cup water. Cover and cook over low heat until the beans are tender (about 30 minutes).

Transfer the vinegar and spices to the container of a blender and blend to a smooth paste. Add to the cooked mung beans, along with the sauteed onion. Stir and cook for 5 minutes. Serve hot.

Yield: Serves 4 with other dishes.

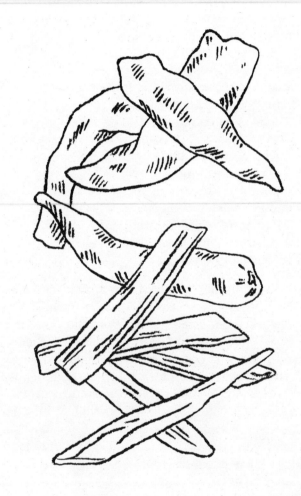

# Kidney Beans in Onion-Tomato Sauce

## *Rajma*

A popular Punjabi dish, Rajma is quite often eaten with rice and a pickle or salad.

2 medium onions
1/2-inch piece fresh ginger
4 cloves garlic
3 tablespoons vegetable oil
1/2 teaspoon cumin seeds
2 medium tomatoes, chopped coarsely
Salt, to taste
1/4 teaspoon cayenne pepper
1/2 teaspoon ground coriander seeds
1/2 teaspoon ground cumin seeds
1/2 teaspoon freshly ground black pepper
3 cups cooked kidney beans, drained (save 1 cup cooking or canned liquid)

Chop the onions finely. Grate the ginger and garlic. In a large heavy-bottomed skillet over medium heat, warm the oil. Add the cumin. When it darkens (1 to 2 seconds), add the grated ginger and garlic. Cook for 1 minute, then add the chopped onions and saute until browned (about 10 minutes). Add the tomatoes, salt, cayenne, coriander, cumin, and black pepper. Cook until the tomatoes are soft (about 5 minutes). Add the kidney beans along with 1 cup of their cooking liquid. Reduce the heat to low, cover, and cook for 7 to 8 minutes. Serve hot.

Yield: Serves 4 with other dishes.

# Chickpeas with Onions and Tomatoes

## *Chole*

Everyone seems to be won over by this dish. Those familiar with bland chickpea preparations love this spicy creation. You can serve it stuffed in pita bread pockets or use it as a topping for crackers.

2 medium onions
3/4-inch piece fresh ginger
6 cloves garlic
4 tablespoons vegetable oil
1 teaspoon cumin seeds
1 bay leaf
1/2-inch stick cinnamon
2 medium tomatoes, chopped coarsely
1/2 teaspoon ground coriander seeds
1/2 teaspoon ground turmeric
Salt, to taste
1/4 teaspoon cayenne pepper
3 cups cooked chickpeas, drained
1/2 teaspoon *garam masala*
1 tablespoon lemon juice

Chop the onions finely. Grate the ginger and garlic. In a large heavy-bottomed skillet over medium heat, warm the oil. Add the cumin, bay leaf, and cinnamon. When the spices darken (1 to 2 seconds), add the grated ginger and garlic. Cook for 1 minute, then add the chopped onions and saute until golden brown (12 to 15 minutes). Add the tomatoes, coriander, turmeric, salt, and cayenne. Cook until the tomatoes are softened (about 5 minutes). Add the chickpeas, cover, reduce the heat to low, and cook for 10 minutes. Mix in the *garam masala* and lemon juice. Serve hot.

Yield: Serves 4 with other dishes.

# Chickpeas with Cottage Cheese

## *Paneer Chole*

If you wish, the homemade cottage cheese can be replaced by chopped fresh tomatoes, onions, cucumbers, and coriander leaves.

**1 recipe homemade cottage cheese**
**Vegetable oil, for deep-frying**
**2 medium onions**
**4 cloves garlic**
**1/2-inch piece fresh ginger**
**4 tablespoons vegetable oil**
**1/2 teaspoon whole cumin seeds**
**1 bay leaf**
**1/4 teaspoon ground roasted cumin seeds**
**1/4 teaspoon ground cumin seeds**
**1/2 teaspoon ground coriander seeds**
**1/2 teaspoon freshly ground black pepper**
**Salt, to taste**
**1/4 teaspoon cayenne pepper**
**1/2 cup water**
**1 teaspoon tamarind paste *or* 2 tablespoons lemon juice**
**1 medium cooked potato, peeled and diced into 1/2-inch cubes**
**3 cups cooked chickpeas, drained**
**1/2 teaspoon *garam masala***

Cut the cottage cheese into 1/2-inch cubes. Warm the oil for deep-frying over medium heat. Fry the cheese cubes until lightly browned; drain and set aside.

Mince the onions, garlic, and ginger together in a food processor or blender. In a large heavy-bottomed skillet over medium heat, warm the 4 tablespoons oil. Add the whole cumin seeds and bay leaf. When the spices darken (1 to 2 seconds), add the minced onion mixture. Saute until the onions are well browned (about 20 minutes), reducing the heat if necessary. Add the whole roasted cumin seeds, ground cumin seeds, coriander, black pepper, salt, and cayenne. Reduce the heat to low and saute for 1 minute. Add the water, tamarind paste (if using lemon juice, add it just before serving), cheese cubes, potato, and chickpeas. Stir gently and cook for 5 to 7 minutes. Mix in the *garam masala* and lemon juice (if using it) and serve.

Yield: Serves 4 with other dishes.

# Vegetables

Because India is largely a country of vegetarians, almost every meal features vegetables. Unlike a Western meal, which is often centered around a meat entree, Indian meals frequently have vegetables as the main dish. In most northern Indian homes, breakfast is usually a hearty meal of *puris* (deep-fried wheat bread) and *alu sabzi* (potatoes with onions and yogurt), or of *parathas* (shallow-fried wheat bread) served with a vegetable dish. In the South, *upma* (a dish of semolina and mixed vegetables) or *idli sambhar* (fermented rice cakes served with lentils and vegetables) is often eaten. Lunch and dinner are also a vegetable and a *dal* eaten with rice or bread, and in-between there are snacks, such as *pakoras* (vegetable fritters), to munch on. Even dessert is often made from a vegetable, such as *Gajar Ka Halva* (grated carrots cooked in milk and nuts).

An abundance of vegetables is grown in India, many varieties not found outside the country and having no English name. Most housewives buy their vegetables fresh every day from vendors who walk the streets at frequent intervals during the morning wheeling pushcarts piled high with seasonal produce. In this age of multistoried buildings, it is not uncommon to see baskets dangling at the end of long ropes lowered from the balcony of the fifth floor for the vendor to fill with fresh produce.

Because vegetables are used extensively in almost every meal, the housewife uses her creativity in preparing them in many different ways. Thus, the same vegetable can be made into a quick stir-fry, put in a sauce, or turned into crepes, dumplings, fritters, raitas, pickles, or relishes. Since each region has its own style of cooking with its own distinctive spicing, the variety of vegetable preparations is endless.

# Beans in Fennel-Yogurt Sauce
## *Sem Saunfwali*

This is an original recipe based on a dish I had at a French-Canadian restaurant, then adapted to reflect the Kashmiri style of cooking. I like to serve it with Chicken in Sour Cream and Nuts and Pan-Broiled Leavened Bread.

1 pound wax or green beans
1/2-inch piece fresh ginger
5 tablespoons plain yogurt
1 1/2 teaspoons ground fennel seeds
1/2 teaspoon coarsely crushed black pepper
1/4 teaspoon ground turmeric
Salt, to taste
1/4 teaspoon cayenne pepper
2 teaspoons water
2 tablespoons vegetable oil
1/2 teaspoon cumin seeds
Pinch crushed asafoetida (optional)

Trim the beans and cut them into 1-inch lengths. Grate the ginger. In a small bowl mix the yogurt, fennel seeds, black pepper, turmeric, salt, cayenne, and the water; set aside.

In a large heavy-bottomed skillet over medium heat, warm the oil. Add the cumin and asafoetida (if used). When the spices darken (1 to 2 seconds), add the grated ginger. Cook for 1 minute, then add the cut beans and reserved yogurt mixture. Reduce the heat to low, cover, and cook for 30 to 35 minutes. Uncover, increase the heat to high, and boil down the sauce for 5 to 7 minutes. The beans should be tender and coated with a thick sauce. Serve hot.

Yield: Serves 4 with other dishes.

# Cabbage with Black-Eyed Peas

## *Bundgobhi Lobhiyewali*

Whenever there was occasion for my father to cook, he would rustle up cabbage with black-eyed peas with a lot of singing and clanging of pots. We often ate this dish with a *dal*, rice, and *chapatis*. It can be used to stuff Potatoes in Puff Pastry. You can also stir-fry ground meat along with it.

1 medium cabbage
2 medium onions
1/2-inch piece fresh ginger
4 tablespoons vegetable oil
1 teaspoon cumin seeds
Salt, to taste
1/4 teaspoon cayenne pepper
1/2 teaspoon ground turmeric
1 cup cooked black-eyed peas, drained
1/2 teaspoon *garam masala*
Dash lemon juice

Halve the cabbage, core it, and slice it into long, thin shreds. Slice the onions into thin half rounds. Grate the ginger. In a large heavy-bottomed skillet over medium heat, warm the oil. Add the cumin. When it darkens (1 to 2 seconds), add the grated ginger. Cook for 1 minute, then add the sliced onions and saute until lightly browned (about 8 minutes). Add the cabbage, salt, cayenne, and turmeric. Stir, cover, reduce the heat to low, and cook until the cabbage is just done (about 20 minutes). Add the black-eyed peas, cover, and cook for another 5 minutes. Mix in the *garam masala* and serve with lemon juice.

Yield: Serves 4 with other dishes.

# Cabbage in Yogurt with Onions

## *Bundgobhi Khatti*

1 medium cabbage
1 cup plain yogurt
2 cups water
1/2-inch piece fresh ginger
2 medium onions
2 tablespoons vegetable oil
1/2 teaspoon cumin seeds
1/2 teaspoon black mustard seeds
8 to 10 dried curry leaves
1/2 teaspoon ground turmeric
1/2 teaspoon ground coriander seeds
1/2 teaspoon freshly ground black pepper
Salt, to taste
1/4 teaspoon cayenne pepper

Halve the cabbage and core it; slice each half into long, thin shreds. In a large bowl beat the yogurt with a spoon until smooth and add the water. Stir again, add the shredded cabbage, and soak it for 30 minutes.

Meanwhile, grate the ginger, and slice the onions into thin half rounds. In a large heavy-bottomed skillet over medium heat, warm the oil. Add the cumin, mustard seeds, and curry leaves. As soon as the seeds splutter, add the grated ginger. Cook for 1 minute, then add the sliced onions and saute until browned (10 to 12 minutes). Reduce the heat to low and add the turmeric, coriander, black pepper, salt, and cayenne; mix well. Remove the cabbage from its marinade with a slotted spoon and add it to the pan, reserving the marinade for another use. Increase the heat to high and stir-fry the cabbage for 10 minutes, adding 1 to 2 spoonfuls of the marinade to prevent sticking, if necessary. Serve hot.

Yield: Serves 4 with other dishes.

# Cauliflower Stuffed with Onions

## *Gobhi Mazedar*

My father-in-law, an enthusiastic cook, once made this dish for me. His recipes are simple, involving a minimum of frying or sauteing, and the results are always delicious.

1 medium cauliflower (1 1/2 pounds)
2 medium onions
1/2-inch piece fresh ginger
4 cloves garlic
2 medium tomatoes
5 tablespoons plain yogurt
1 teaspoon ground coriander seeds
1/2 teaspoon ground cumin seeds
1/4 teaspoon ground turmeric
Salt, to taste
1/4 teaspoon cayenne pepper
1/2 teaspoon *garam masala*
Butter, to top cauliflower

Remove the leaves and bottom stalk from the cauliflower. Select a large pot that can hold the whole cauliflower head and pour in 3 inches of water. Cover and bring to a boil. Place the cauliflower in the pot bottom down, cover, and cook over medium heat for 15 minutes.

In the container of a blender or food processor, mince together the onion, ginger, garlic, and 1 tomato. Transfer to a large bowl. Mix in the yogurt, coriander, cumin, turmeric, salt, cayenne, and *garam masala*.

Preheat the oven to 400°F. Remove the cauliflower from the water and pat it dry with a paper towel. Allow to cool slightly. Place it in a deep, greased casserole. Stuff half the onion-spice mixture in all the spaces between the florets and spread the remaining mixture over the top of the cauliflower. Slice the remaining tomato into rings and arrange them evenly over the cauliflower. Dot it with a little butter and bake uncovered until the top is browned and the cauliflower is cooked through (about 30 minutes).

For each serving, cut out a portion of the cauliflower, place it on a plate, and spoon some of the sauce from the bottom of the casserole over the top.

Yield: Serves 4 with other dishes.

# Cauliflower in Tomato-Yogurt Sauce

## *Gobhi Mughlai*

1 large cauliflower (about 1 1/2 pounds)
Vegetable oil, for deep-frying
2 medium onions
1-inch piece fresh ginger
4 cloves garlic
3 tablespoons vegetable oil
1/2 teaspoon cumin seeds
1 bay leaf
1/2-inch stick cinnamon
2 medium tomatoes, chopped coarsely
4 tablespoons plain yogurt, beaten with a spoon
1/2 teaspoon ground turmeric
Salt, to taste
1/4 teaspoon cayenne pepper
1/4 cup water
1/4 teaspoon *garam masala*
1/4 teaspoon ground cinnamon

Divide the cauliflower into florets no bigger than 1 to 1 1/2 inches at the top. Heat the oil for deep-frying over medium-high heat. Fry the florets until golden brown, and set aside.

In the container of a food processor or blender, mince the onions, ginger, and garlic together. In a large skillet over medium heat, warm the 3 tablespoons oil. Add the cumin, bay leaf, and cinnamon stick. When the spices darken (1 to 2 seconds), add the minced onion mixture and saute until golden brown (12 to 15 minutes). Add the tomatoes and cook until soft (about 5 minutes). Add the yogurt, mix well, and cook for 5 minutes. Add the turmeric, salt, cayenne, and fried cauliflower florets, and toss gently to coat with the sauce. Stir in the water, cover, reduce the heat to low, and cook for 8 to 10 minutes. Gently mix in the *garam masala* and ground cinnamon. Serve hot.

Yield: Serves 4 with other dishes.

# Minced Cauliflower with Onions

## *Gobhi Ka Keema*

1 medium cauliflower (1 1/2 pounds)
7 tablespoons vegetable oil
1/2-inch piece fresh ginger
3 cloves garlic
2 medium onions
1/2-inch stick cinnamon
1/2 teaspoon cumin seeds
Salt, to taste
1/4 teaspoon cayenne pepper
5 tablespoons canned crushed tomatoes in thick puree
5 tablespoons plain yogurt, beaten with a spoon
1 cup peas
1/2 cup water
1/2 teaspoon *garam masala*

Divide the cauliflower into florets and grate them in a food processor. In a wide-bottomed, preferably nonstick pan over high heat, warm 5 tablespoons of the oil. Add the cauliflower and saute for 10 minutes. Reduce the heat to medium-low and continue cooking for another 30 minutes. Stir it frequently; the cauliflower should be dark brown.

Grate the ginger and garlic. Chop the onions finely. In a large heavy-bottomed skillet over medium heat, warm the remaining 2 tablespoons oil. Add the cinnamon and cumin. When the spices darken (1 to 2 seconds), add the grated ginger and garlic. Cook for 1 minute, add the chopped onions, and saute until well browned (about 15 minutes). Reduce the heat to low, and add the salt, cayenne, and tomatoes. Mix well, then add the yogurt. Cook for 2 minutes, then add the peas and the water. Increase the heat to high and bring to a boil, then add the sauteed cauliflower, cover, reduce the heat to low, and cook for 15 minutes, stirring occasionally. Mix in the *garam masala* and serve hot.

Yield: Serves 4 with other dishes.

# Corn Curry

## *Makai Kari*

Traditionally made with corn, this dish can also be made with mixed vegetables.

**2 tablespoons broken cashew nut pieces**
**1 tablespoon roasted, skinless peanuts**
**1 tablespoon unsweetened dried coconut flakes**
**1 teaspoon white poppy seeds**
**1 medium onion**
**1/4-inch piece fresh ginger**
**2 large cloves garlic**
**1 green chilli (deseeded if desired)**
**3 tablespoons vegetable oil**
**1/2 teaspoon black mustard seeds**
**8 to 10 dried curry leaves**
**1 teaspoon white sesame seeds**
**1 medium tomato**
**1/4 teaspoon ground coriander seeds**
**1/4 teaspoon ground cumin seeds**
**1/2 teaspoon freshly ground black pepper**
**1/2 teaspoon ground turmeric**
**Salt, to taste**
**1/4 teaspoon sugar**
**3 cups corn kernels**
**1/4 cup yogurt diluted with 1/4 cup water**

In a large heavy-bottomed skillet over low heat, dry-roast together the cashews, peanuts, coconut, and poppy seeds until the cashews have brown specks (a few minutes). Remove from the heat and let cool slightly. In the container of a food processor or blender, coarsely chop together the onion, ginger, and garlic. Add the chilli and roasted cashew mixture and mince well.

In a large heavy-bottomed skillet, warm the oil over medium heat. Add the mustard seeds, curry leaves, and sesame seeds. As soon as the mustard seeds splutter, add the minced onion mixture and saute until lightly browned (7 to 8 minutes). Whirl the tomato to a puree in the blender. Add it to the pan with the coriander, cumin, black pepper, turmeric, salt, and sugar, and cook for 5 to 6 minutes. Add the corn, mix well, and cook for 2 minutes. Stir in the diluted yogurt, cover, reduce the heat to low, and cook for 20 minutes, stirring occasionally. Serve hot.

Yield: Serves 4 with other dishes.

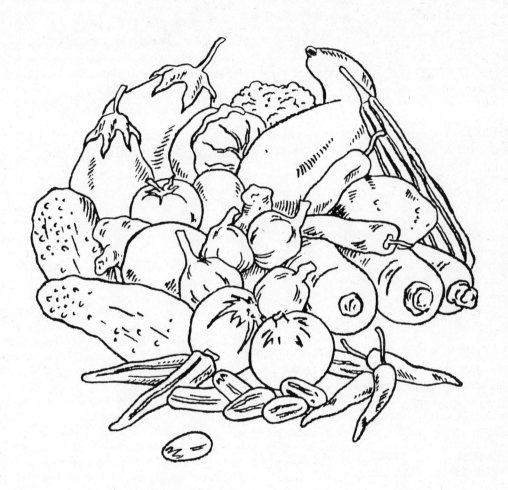

# Eggplant with Onions and Cottage Cheese

## *Paneer Bhare Baingan*

Some of my friends claim that the only way they can eat eggplant is when it is cooked Indian style. Here is a dish that appeals to them. You may serve it with a simple salad and crusty French bread.

**2 medium eggplants (about 1 1/2 pounds total)**
**2 medium onions**
**1/2-inch piece fresh ginger**
**2 large cloves garlic**
**3 tablespoons vegetable oil**
**1/2 teaspoon whole cumin seeds**
**2 medium tomatoes, chopped coarsely**
**4 tablespoons plain yogurt**
**1/2 teaspoon ground coriander seeds**
**1/2 teaspoon ground cumin seeds**
**1/2 teaspoon *garam masala***
**Salt, to taste**
**1/4 teaspoon cayenne pepper**
**1/2 cup cottage cheese (store-bought is fine)**

Cut the eggplants in half lengthwise. Place them cut side down on a greased baking sheet and bake at 350°F for 25 to 30 minutes. Meanwhile, chop the onions finely and grate the ginger and garlic.

In a large heavy-bottomed skillet over medium heat, warm the oil. Add the whole cumin seeds. When they darken (1 to 2 seconds), add the grated ginger and garlic. Saute for 1 minute, then add the chopped onions and saute until lightly browned (7 to 8 minutes). Add the tomatoes and cook until soft (about 5 minutes).

Scoop out the insides of the baked eggplant halves, leaving a 1/4-inch-thick shell. Chop up the insides finely and add to the onion mixture. Reduce the heat to low, cover, and cook for 7 to 8 minutes.

Beat the yogurt with a spoon and add to the eggplant mixture, stirring constantly. Add the coriander, ground cumin seeds, *garam masala*, salt, and cayenne. Mix well and remove from the heat. Let cool for 5 minutes, then mix in the cottage cheese.

Preheat the oven to 350°F. Lightly dust the insides of the eggplant shells with salt. Stuff them generously with the cottage cheese mixture. Bake uncovered for 35 to 40 minutes. If the tops of the eggplant seem to be burning or are getting too dry, cover them with aluminum foil. Remove from the oven and serve hot.

Yield: Serves 4 with other dishes.

# Eggplant in Onion-Tomato Sauce

## *Bharvan Baingan Rasedar*

You can also make this dish without the sauce. Just place the stuffed eggplant in a little oil and cook covered until tender, turning occasionally to ensure even cooking.

1/2-inch piece fresh ginger
3 large cloves garlic
2 medium onions
3 tablespoons vegetable oil
1/4 teaspoon whole cumin seeds
2 large tomatoes, chopped coarsely
4 baby Italian eggplants (about 1 pound)
1/4 cup water

*Stuffing*

1/2 teaspoon ground coriander seeds
1/4 teaspoon ground cumin seeds
1/2 teaspoon *garam masala*
1/2 teaspoon ground fennel seeds
1/4 teaspoon freshly ground black pepper
1/4 teaspoon cayenne pepper
Salt, to taste
1 teaspoon water

Grate the ginger and garlic. Finely chop the onions. In a large heavy-bottomed skillet over medium heat, warm the oil. Add the whole cumin seeds. When they darken (1 to 2 seconds), add the grated ginger and garlic. Cook for 1 minute, then add the chopped onions and saute until lightly browned (7 to 8 minutes). Add the tomatoes and cook until softened (about 5 minutes).

Meanwhile, wash and dry the eggplants well. Do not trim the stems. Make a deep lengthwise slit in the eggplants, leaving about 1/4 inch intact near both ends. Take care not to slice through them.

To prepare the stuffing, make a paste of all the spices and the 1 teaspoon water. Stuff this mixture into the eggplants.

Pour the 1/4 cup water into the onion mixture, then place the eggplants on top, side by side. Cover tightly, reduce the heat to very low, and cook until the eggplants are tender (about 30 minutes), stirring occasionally during the last 15 minutes of cooking time. To serve, place an eggplant on each plate and spoon some sauce over the top.

Yield: Serves 4 with other dishes.

# Eggplant with Tomatoes and Mustard

## *Sorse Begun*

The flavors of mustard and eggplant blend together exceptionally well in this dish. For a richer effect, the eggplant may be deep-fried before being added to the sauce. Cauliflower florets can also be used in place of the eggplant. My friend Bansari, who gave me this recipe, likes to serve this dish with a *dal* and Pan-Broiled Wheat Bread.

1 1/2 tablespoons black mustard seeds
2 tablespoons water
1/2-inch piece fresh ginger
2 medium onions, chopped fine
3 tablespoons vegetable oil
8 to 10 dried curry leaves
2 medium tomatoes, chopped coarsely
1/2 teaspoon ground turmeric
1/2 teaspoon ground coriander seeds
Salt, to taste
1 large eggplant (about 1 1/4 pounds), cut into
   3/4-inch cubes

Soak the mustard seeds in 1/2 cup water for 30 minutes. Discard the water. Blend the mustard seeds and 2 tablespoons of water and the ginger to a smooth paste. Set aside. Chop the onions finely.

In a large heavy-bottomed skillet over medium heat, warm the oil. Add the curry leaves. When they darken (1 to 2 seconds), add the chopped onions and saute until lightly browned (7 to 8 minutes). Reduce the heat to low and add the mustard-ginger paste. Saute for about 3 minutes. Add the tomatoes and cook until softened (about 5 minutes). Add the turmeric, coriander, salt, and eggplant. Cover, reduce the heat to very low, and cook until the eggplant is tender (20 to 25 minutes). Serve hot.

Yield: Serves 4 with other dishes.

# Eggplant in Garlic-Herb Sauce

## *Hare Baingan*

For crisper eggplant, cook it uncovered over medium heat, using more oil if necessary.

2 medium eggplants (about 1 1/4 pounds total)
2 medium onions
1/2-inch piece fresh ginger
10 cloves garlic
1/2 cup fresh mint leaves
1/2 cup fresh coriander leaves
10 dried curry leaves (optional)
1 green chilli, deseeded, if desired
1 teaspoon ground coriander seeds
1/2 teaspoon ground turmeric
Salt, to taste
2 medium tomatoes, chopped finely
6 tablespoons vegetable oil
2 tablespoons lemon juice

Wash and dry the eggplants. Slice them into rounds of medium thickness. Place the onions, ginger, garlic, mint, coriander leaves, curry leaves (if used), and chilli in the container of a food processor or blender and blend to a slightly coarse paste. Transfer to a large bowl and mix in the ground coriander seeds, turmeric, and salt. Prick the eggplant slices with a knife or fork and rub each side with the spice paste.

In a wide-bottomed, preferably nonstick pan, warm the oil over medium heat. Arrange the eggplant slices in a single layer. Dot each slice with a few pieces of tomato. Cover, reduce the heat to low, and cook for 8 minutes. Carefully flip the slices (with the tomatoes under each slice now) and cook covered until the eggplant is tender (another 7 to 8 minutes), adding more oil if necessary. Sprinkle with the lemon juice and serve.

Yield: Serves 4 with other dishes.

# Eggplant with Chickpeas
## *Kathrikai Kadale*

This unusual eggplant dish has chickpeas for added nutrition. Cauliflower or broccoli could be cooked in this sauce, but without the chickpeas. You could serve it with Chicken in Coconut Milk and Deep-Fried Wheat Bread.

1 medium eggplant (about 1 pound)
Vegetable oil, for deep-frying
1-inch piece fresh ginger
2 cloves garlic
2 medium onions
3 tablespoons vegetable oil
8 dried curry leaves
1/2 teaspoon cumin seeds
1/2 teaspoon black mustard seeds
1 teaspoon white sesame seeds
2 teaspoons unsweetened desiccated coconut
   powder
4 tablespoons plain yogurt
1/4 teaspoon ground turmeric
Salt, to taste
1/4 teaspoon cayenne pepper
1 1/2 cups cooked, drained chickpeas
1/2 teaspoon *garam masala*
1 tablespoon lemon juice

Cut the eggplant into 2-inch wedges. Warm the oil for deep-frying over medium-high heat and fry the eggplant pieces until lightly browned and tender. Drain on paper towels for at least 10 minutes. Grate the ginger and garlic. Chop the onions finely.

In a large heavy-bottomed skillet over medium heat, warm the 3 tablespoons oil. Add the curry leaves, cumin, mustard seeds, sesame seeds, and coconut. When they darken (1 to 2 seconds), add the grated ginger and garlic. Cook for 1 minute,

then add the chopped onions and saute until lightly browned (about 8 minutes). Reduce the heat to low, beat the yogurt with a spoon, and add it to the pan. Cook for 2 minutes, then add the turmeric, salt, and cayenne. Add the chickpeas and mix well, then add the eggplant and toss gently to mix with the sauce. Cover and cook for 5 minutes. Mix in the *garam masala* and lemon juice. Serve hot.

Yield: Serves 4 with other dishes.

# Okra with Chickpea Flour

## *Bhindi Nu Shak*

Most Gujaratis are strict vegetarians, and add protein to their diet by using chickpea flour, yogurt, nuts, and beans in their preparations. Many of their dishes are lightly flavored with sugar and lemon juice, making them temptingly sweet and sour.

**3/4 pound fresh okra**
**1/2-inch piece fresh ginger**
**3 large cloves garlic**
**1 tablespoon vegetable oil**
**Pinch crushed asafoetida (optional)**
**1/2 teaspoon black mustard seeds**
**6 to 7 dried curry leaves**
**Salt, to taste**
**1/3 cup chickpea flour**
**1/2 teaspoon ground coriander seeds**
**1/2 teaspoon ground cumin seeds**
**1/4 teaspoon cayenne pepper**
**1/2 teaspoon ground turmeric**
**1/4 teaspoon *garam masala***
**1/2 teaspoon sugar**
**2 tablespoons lemon juice**

Wash the okra and pat completely dry with a paper towel. Snip off both ends and cut the okra into 1/2-inch pieces. Grate the ginger and garlic. In a large heavy-bottomed skillet over medium heat, warm the oil. Add the asafoetida (if used), mustard seeds, and curry leaves. As soon as the mustard seeds splutter, add the okra pieces and salt, cover, reduce the heat to very low, and cook for 9 minutes.

Meanwhile, in a heavy-bottomed skillet over low heat, dry-roast the chickpea flour until it turns a few shades darker and smells fragrant (5 to 7 minutes). Transfer it to a small bowl and mix in the coriander, cumin, cayenne, turmeric, *garam masala*,

and sugar. Sprinkle over the cooked okra. Add the lemon juice and gently toss the mixture. Cook covered until the okra is tender (about 6 minutes), stirring occasionally. Serve hot.

Yield: Serves 4 with other dishes.

# Cottage Cheese with Peas
## *Matar Paneer*

The cottage cheese absorbs the flavor of the sauce and becomes soft and spicy. This dish is a perfect accompaniment to Chicken in Sour Cream and Nuts or Shrimp with Fenugreek. Serve an Indian bread of your choice with it.

**1 recipe homemade cottage cheese**
**Vegetable oil, for deep-frying, plus 2 tablespoons**
  **vegetable oil**
**2 medium onions**
**1/2-inch piece fresh ginger**
**3 cloves garlic**
**1/2 teaspoon cumin seeds**
**1 large tomato**
**1/2 teaspoon ground turmeric**
**Salt, to taste**
**1/4 teaspoon cayenne pepper**
**1/2 teaspoon ground coriander seeds**
**1 1/2 cups peas, fresh or frozen**
**1 cup water**
**1/2 teaspoon *garam masala***

Dice the cottage cheese into 1/2-inch cubes. Warm the oil for deep-frying over medium-high heat and gently fry the cheese cubes until they are lightly browned on all sides. Drain on paper towels and set aside.

In the container of a blender or food processor, mince together the onions, ginger, and garlic. In a large heavy-bottomed skillet over medium heat, warm the 2 tablespoons oil. Add the cumin. When it darkens (1 to 2 seconds), add the minced onion mixture and saute until lightly browned (about 8 minutes). Whirl the tomato to a puree in the blender, add it to the pan, and cook for about 8 minutes. Add the turmeric, salt, cayenne, and coriander and cook for 1 minute more. Add the peas, fried cottage cheese cubes, and the water. Cover, increase the heat to high, bring the contents of the pan to a boil, reduce the heat to low, and cook for 15 minutes. Remove from the heat, gently mix in the *garam masala*, and serve.

Yield: Serves 4 with other dishes.

# Cottage Cheese, Peas, and Nuts in Creamy Tomato Sauce

## *Kaju Matar Paneer*

1 recipe homemade cottage cheese
Vegetable oil, for deep-frying, plus 2 tablespoons vegetable oil
2/3 cup cashew nuts
1-inch piece fresh ginger
2 large cloves garlic
1/2 teaspoon cumin seeds
1 1/2 cups canned crushed tomatoes in thick puree
Salt, to taste
1/4 teaspoon cayenne pepper
1/4 teaspoon ground turmeric
1 1/2 cups peas, fresh or frozen
1 teaspoon *garam masala*
1/4 cup whipping cream
Fresh coriander leaves, for garnish

Dice the cottage cheese into 1/2-inch cubes. Warm the oil for deep-frying over medium-high heat and fry the cheese cubes until they are golden brown on all sides. Remove with a slotted spoon and drain on paper towels. Deep-fry the cashews until they are golden brown; drain on paper towels and set aside.

Grate the ginger and garlic. In a large heavy-bottomed skillet over medium heat, warm the 2 tablespoons oil. Add the cumin. When it darkens (1 to 2 seconds), add the grated ginger and garlic. Cook for 1 minute, then reduce the heat to low and add the tomatoes, salt, cayenne, turmeric, fried cashews, fried cottage cheese cubes, and peas. Cover and cook for 20 minutes. Mix in the *garam masala* and cream. Remove from the heat and serve garnished with coriander leaves.

Yield: Serves 4 with other dishes.

# Peas with Ginger and Cumin

## *Matar Ki Ghugri*

A simple dish flavored with ginger and cumin, this complements a Western meal as easily as it does an Indian one. My mother often serves it at family brunches with Stuffed Wheat Bread. It can be used as a stuffing for baked tomatoes. Or the peas can be mashed coarsely and stuffed into Deep-Fried Wheat Bread or Shallow-Fried Wheat Bread.

1/2-inch piece fresh ginger
1 green chilli
2 tablespoons vegetable oil
Pinch crushed asafoetida (optional)
1 teaspoon cumin seeds
3 cups peas, fresh or frozen
1/2 cup water
1/4 teaspoon sugar
Salt, to taste
3 tablespoons chopped fresh coriander leaves
1 tablespoon lemon juice

Grate the ginger and finely chop the chilli. In a large heavy-bottomed skillet over medium heat, warm the oil. Add the asafoetida (if used) and cumin. When the spices darken (1 to 2 seconds), add the grated ginger and chopped chilli. Cook for 1 minute, then add the peas, the water, sugar, and salt. Reduce the heat to medium-low, cover, and cook until the peas are tender. Uncover, increase the heat to high, and boil off any remaining liquid. Mix in the coriander and lemon juice and serve hot.

Yield: Serves 4 with other dishes.

# Peas with Mushrooms
## *Kumbhi Matar*

This versatile dish can be served for dinner with Pan-Broiled Wheat Bread and a dal, and the leftovers either stuffed in pita bread pockets or in an omelette, or as a substitute filling for Potatoes in Puff Pastry.

2 medium onions
1/2-inch piece fresh ginger
3 tablespoons vegetable oil
1 teaspoon cumin seeds
1-inch stick cinnamon
2 cardamom pods
4 cloves
3/4 pound fresh mushrooms, sliced thickly
2 medium tomatoes, chopped coarsely
2 cups peas, fresh or frozen
Salt, to taste
1/4 teaspoon cayenne pepper
1/2 teaspoon freshly ground black pepper

Slice the onions finely. Grate the ginger. In a large heavy-bottomed skillet over medium heat, warm the oil. Add the cumin, cinnamon, cardamom, and cloves. When the spices darken (1 to 2 seconds), add the grated ginger. Cook for 1 minute, then add the sliced onions and saute until lightly browned (7 to 8 minutes). Add the mushrooms and saute for 5 minutes. Add the tomatoes, peas, salt, cayenne, and black pepper. Stir, reduce the heat to low, cover, and cook until the peas are just tender (about 15 minutes). Uncover, increase the heat to high, and boil down the sauce for about 5 minutes. Serve hot.

Yield: Serves 4 with other dishes.

# Spicy Green Peas
## *Pacha Patani Shundal*

Poppy seeds and coconut are ground into the sauce of this dish, giving it a pleasant nutty flavor. These peas could also be served with Lamb with Spices and Shallow-Fried Wheat Bread.

1 1/2 tablespoons white poppy seeds
3 cloves garlic
2 medium onions
1/2-inch piece fresh ginger
2 tablespoons grated fresh coconut
3 tablespoons vegetable oil
1/2 teaspoon black mustard seeds
10 dried curry leaves
2 tablespoons plain yogurt, beaten with a spoon
Salt, to taste
1/4 teaspoon cayenne pepper
1 teaspoon ground coriander seeds
1/2 teaspoon freshly ground black pepper
1/4 teaspoon ground turmeric
2 1/2 cups peas, fresh or frozen

Soak the poppy seeds in water for 20 minutes, then drain. In the container of a food processor or blender, grind the soaked poppy seeds, garlic, onions, ginger, and coconut to a fine paste, adding a few drops of water if necessary.

In a large heavy-bottomed skillet over medium heat, warm the oil. Add the mustard seeds and curry leaves. As soon as the seeds splutter, add the poppy seed paste. Cook for 10 minutes, then reduce the heat to low and cook until fairly browned (about 5 minutes more). Add the yogurt and cook for about 7 minutes. Add the salt, cayenne, coriander, black pepper, and turmeric. Cook for 1 minute, then add the peas, mix them well with the sauce, cover, and cook until the peas are tender (about 25 minutes). Serve hot.

Yield: Serves 4 with other dishes.

# Green Bell Peppers Stuffed with Potatoes

*Alu Bhari Mirch*

4 large green bell peppers
6 medium potatoes (2 1/4 pounds total)
2 medium onions
3/4-inch piece fresh ginger
5 tablespoons vegetable oil
1 teaspoon cumin seeds
3/4 teaspoon ground coriander seeds
3/4 teaspoon *garam masala*
Salt, to taste
1/4 teaspoon cayenne pepper
1 tablespoon lemon juice

Carefully core the bell peppers by cutting around the stalks; remove and discard the seeds and save the caps. Cook the potatoes in their skins until tender. Peel and mash coarsely. Chop the onions finely. Grate the ginger.

In a large heavy-bottomed skillet over medium heat, warm 2 tablespoons of the oil. Add the cumin. When it darkens (1 to 2 seconds), add the grated ginger. Cook for 1 minute, then add the chopped onions and saute for 10 minutes. Add the coriander, *garam masala*, salt, and cayenne; mix well, then add the mashed potatoes. Cook for 5 minutes, remove from the heat, and add the lemon juice. Stuff this mixture generously into the bell peppers. Replace their caps.

In a large wide-bottomed nonstick skillet over medium heat, warm the remaining 3 tablespoons oil. Reduce the heat to low and carefully place the stuffed peppers side by side in the pan. Cover and cook until the peppers are tender and speckled with brown on all sides (about 30 minutes), turning them occasionally. Serve hot.

Yield: Serves 4 with other dishes.

# Green Bell Peppers with Potatoes

*Alu Mirch Ki Sabzi*

Here is a simple, delicious way to cook green bell peppers. You can serve them with any dal of your choice, or with Baked Chicken and Shallow-Fried Wheat Bread. They also make a good side dish in a Western meal.

5 small green bell peppers (about 1 pound total)
1 large onion
1/2-inch piece fresh ginger
2 tablespoons vegetable oil
1/2 teaspoon cumin seeds
Pinch crushed asafoetida (optional)
1 medium potato, peeled and diced into 3/4-inch cubes
Salt, to taste
1/4 teaspoon cayenne pepper
Dash lemon juice (optional)

Deseed the bell peppers and cut them into 1-inch pieces. Slice the onion into thin half rounds. Grate the ginger. In a large heavy-bottomed skillet over medium heat, warm the oil. Add the cumin and asafoetida (if used). When the spices darken (1 to 2 seconds), add the grated ginger and cook for 1 minute. Add the sliced onion and saute until lightly browned (7 to 8 minutes). Add the potato, cover, reduce the heat to low, and cook about 8 minutes. Add the chopped bell peppers, salt, and cayenne. Mix well, cover, and cook for 15 to 20 minutes. Serve with lemon juice, if desired.

Yield: Serves 4 with other dishes.

# Green Bell Peppers with Vegetables and Cottage Cheese

## *Paneer Bhari Mirch*

The green and red colors in this dish make it a spectacular sight on the table. You could also substitute zucchini or eggplant for the bell peppers and serve it with Chicken in Sour Cream and Nuts and Shallow-Fried Wheat Bread.

**1 medium onion**
**2 tablespoons vegetable oil**
**1/2 teaspoon cumin seeds**
**1 1/2 cups frozen chopped mixed vegetables, thawed and drained**
**Salt, to taste**
**6 tablespoons cottage cheese (store-bought is fine)**
**1/2-inch piece fresh ginger**
**3 cloves garlic**
**1 green chilli *or* 1/4 teaspoon cayenne pepper**
**2 cups fresh tomato puree**
**1/2 teaspoon ground turmeric**
**1/2 teaspoon ground coriander seeds**
**1/2 teaspoon *garam masala***
**1/2 teaspoon sugar**
**4 medium green bell peppers (about 1 pound total)**

Chop the onion finely. In a large heavy-bottomed skillet over medium heat, warm the oil. Add the cumin. When it darkens (1 to 2 seconds), add the chopped onion and saute until lightly browned (about 7 minutes). Add the mixed vegetables and salt, and cook for about 7 minutes. Remove from the heat and allow to cool slightly, then mix in the cottage cheese.

Mince the ginger, garlic, and chilli together in a food processor or blender. Add to the tomato puree along with the turmeric, coriander, *garam masala*,

salt, and sugar. Pour into the bottom of a wide ovenproof dish.

Preheat the oven to 350°F. Slice each bell pepper in half and remove the seeds. Stuff each half generously with the vegetable-cottage cheese mixture and place gently, side by side, on the tomato puree mixture. Bake uncovered for 40 minutes. To serve, place a stuffed pepper half on each plate and spoon some tomato sauce over the top.

Yield: Serves 4 with other dishes.

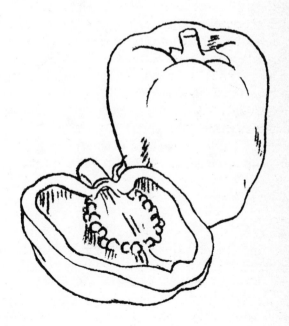

# Potatoes in Coriander-Yogurt Sauce

## *Dhaniye Ke Alu*

This is an excellent dish to serve at parties; it is fragrant, delicious, and easy to prepare. It can be made ahead of time except for the herb sauce, which can be quickly pureed and added just before serving. This dish could be served with Chicken in Tomato Puree and Stuffed Wheat Bread, or mashed and stuffed into Shallow-Fried Wheat Bread or hollowed-out zucchini, which is then baked.

12 small potatoes (about 1 1/2 pounds total)
2 medium onions
3 cloves garlic
3 tablespoons vegetable oil
Pinch crushed asafoetida (optional)
1 bay leaf
1/2 teaspoon cumin seeds
1/2 teaspoon ground coriander seeds
1/2 teaspoon ground turmeric
1/2 teaspoon *garam masala*
Salt, to taste
6 tablespoons plain yogurt
Herb sauce
1/2-inch piece fresh ginger
1 green chilli (deseeded if desired)
3/4 cup fresh coriander leaves and tender upper
   stems
1/4 cup water

Boil the potatoes until tender but not mushy. Peel and set aside. In the container of a blender or food processor, mince together the onions and garlic. In a large heavy-bottomed skillet over medium heat, warm the oil. Add the asafoetida (if used), bay leaf, and cumin. When the spices darken (1 to 2 seconds), add the minced onion mixture and saute until browned (10 to 12 minutes). Reduce the heat to low and add the ground coriander seeds, turmeric, *garam masala*, and salt. Beat the yogurt with a spoon and add it to the pan, stirring constantly. Cook for 2 to 3 minutes, then add the boiled potatoes. Toss them well with the sauce, cover, and cook for 5 minutes.

Make the herb sauce just before serving by pureeing the ginger, chilli, fresh coriander leaves, and the water in the container of a blender or food processor. Add the sauce to the potatoes in the pan, stirring to coat them well, and heat through. Serve hot.

Yield: Serves 4 with other dishes.

# Potatoes in Creamy Yogurt Sauce

## *Dum Alu*

Potatoes are a relatively late addition to the Indian diet, brought by the Portuguese from their South American colonies. The Indians soon adapted this versatile vegetable to their own cuisine, serving it up in numerous delicious ways. In its preparation Dum Alu reflects the Mughlai influence. It is delicious mashed and stuffed into Shallow-Fried Wheat Bread or hollowed-out zucchini, which is then baked. For a lighter dish omit deep-frying the potatoes after boiling them.

**12 small potatoes (about 1 1/2 pounds total)**
**Vegetable oil, for deep-frying**
**2 medium onions**
**1/2-inch piece fresh ginger**
**4 cloves garlic**
**3 tablespoons vegetable oil**
**1 teaspoon cumin seeds**
**1 bay leaf**
**1/2-inch stick cinnamon**
**1 teaspoon ground coriander seeds**
**Salt, to taste**
**1/4 teaspoon cayenne pepper**
**1/2 teaspoon freshly ground black pepper**
**4 tablespoons plain yogurt**
**1/2 teaspoon *garam masala***
**1/2 cup water**
**1 tablespoon whipping cream**

Boil the potatoes until just tender but not mushy. Peel and pat dry with a paper towel. Warm the oil for deep-frying over medium-high heat and fry the potatoes until golden brown on all sides. Prick each potato several times with a toothpick or fork; set aside.

In the container of a blender or food processor, mince together the onions, ginger, and garlic. In a large heavy-bottomed skillet over medium heat, warm the 3 tablespoons oil. Add the cumin, bay leaf, and cinnamon. When the spices darken (1 to 2 seconds), add the onion mixture and saute until well browned (about 15 minutes). Reduce the heat to low and add the coriander, salt, cayenne, and black pepper. Cook for 1 minute. Beat the yogurt with a spoon and gradually add it to the pan, stirring constantly. Cook for 7 to 8 minutes. Mix in the *garam masala* and the water. Add the cooked potatoes and stir to coat with the sauce. Cover the pan, increase the heat to high, and bring to a boil. Reduce the heat to low and cook for 10 minutes. Mix in the cream and serve hot.

Yield: Serves 4 with other dishes.

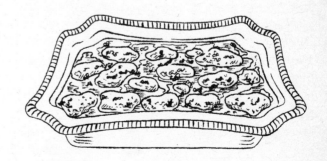

# Potatoes with Scallions
## *Alu Pyaz Ki Sabzi*

This dish from my mother-in-law's repertoire has long been a family favorite. It tastes wonderful with Pan-Broiled Wheat Bread and a dal. It can also be used as a stuffing for Potatoes in Puff Pastry or Parathe or made into croquettes.

**6 bunches green onions (6 in each bunch), including green parts**
**3 medium potatoes**
**2 tablespoons vegetable oil**
**1/2 teaspoon cumin seeds**
**Pinch crushed asafoetida (optional)**
**1/2 teaspoon ground turmeric**
**Salt, to taste**
**1/4 teaspoon cayenne pepper**
**3/4 teaspoon ground coriander seeds**
**1 tablespoon lemon juice**

Cut the green onions into 1/4-inch pieces; set aside. Peel the potatoes and dice them into 1-inch cubes. In a large nonstick pan over medium heat, warm the oil. Add the cumin and asafoetida (if used). When the spices darken (1 to 2 seconds), add the turmeric. Cook for 1 second, then add the diced potatoes. Stir to coat them with the oil and spices, then cover, reduce the heat to low, and cook for 10 minutes.

Add the sliced green onions, salt, cayenne, and coriander to the potatoes. Cover, increase the heat to medium, and cook for 6 to 7 minutes. Uncover the pan and stir until the vegetable is dry and cooked through (about 5 minutes). Mix in the lemon juice and serve.

Yield: Serves 4 with other dishes.

# Potatoes and Peas in Onion-Tomato Sauce
## *Alu Matar*

One of the better known dishes of Uttar Pradesh cuisine, this is a favorite at occasions ranging from a wedding buffet to a family picnic. It goes exceptionally well with Deep-Fried Wheat Bread, a raita, and Pumpkin with Onions and Fenugreek.

**12 small potatoes (about 1 1/2 pounds total)**
**2 medium onions**
**3 cloves garlic**
**1/2-inch piece fresh ginger**
**3 tablespoons vegetable oil**
**Pinch crushed asafoetida (optional)**
**1/2 teaspoon cumin seeds**
**Salt, to taste**
**1/4 teaspoon cayenne pepper**
**1/2 teaspoon ground turmeric**
**2 large tomatoes, chopped coarsely**
**1 cup peas**
**1/4 cup water**
**1/2 teaspoon *garam masala***

Cook the potatoes until tender. Peel and set aside. In the container of a blender or food processor, mince together the onions, garlic, and ginger. In a large heavy-bottomed skillet over medium heat, warm the oil. Add the asafoetida (if used) and cumin. When the spices darken (1 to 2 seconds), add the minced onion mixture and saute until browned (about 12 minutes). Add the salt, cayenne, turmeric, and tomatoes and cook until they soften (about 5 minutes). Add the peas and the water; reduce the heat to low, cover, and cook for 5 minutes. Halve the cooked potatoes if they seem too large. Add them to the pan and cook covered for another 5 minutes. Mix in the *garam masala* just before serving.

Yield: Serves 4 with other dishes.

# Potatoes with Fenugreek
## *Alu Methi*

The potatoes can be coarsely mashed and used as a stuffing for Shallow-Fried Wheat Bread. Or you can substitute diced carrots for the potatoes. They add a pleasant sweetness to the dish. The carrots don't have to be deep-fried and can be added along with the fenugreek leaves.

**4 cups fresh fenugreek leaves**
**2 medium potatoes**
**Vegetable oil, for deep-frying**
**1/2-inch piece fresh ginger**
**2 cloves garlic**
**2 medium onions**
**2 tablespoons vegetable oil**
**1/2 teaspoon cumin seeds**
**Salt, to taste**
**1/4 teaspoon cayenne pepper**
**1/2 teaspoon ground turmeric**
**2 tablespoons lemon juice**

Wash the fenugreek leaves and chop them coarsely; set aside. Dice the potatoes into 1/2-inch cubes. Warm the oil for deep-frying over medium-high heat and fry the potatoes until golden brown on all sides. Drain and set aside.

Grate the ginger and garlic. Finely chop the onions. In a large heavy-bottomed skillet over medium heat, warm the 2 tablespoons oil. Add the cumin. When it darkens (1 to 2 seconds), add the grated ginger and garlic. Cook for 1 minute, then add the chopped onions and saute until golden brown (10 to 12 minutes). Add the salt, cayenne, turmeric, and the chopped fenugreek leaves. Mix well, cover, reduce the heat to low, and cook for 10 minutes. Add the fried potatoes, cover, and cook for 5 minutes. Add the lemon juice and serve.

Yield: Serves 4 with other dishes.

# Pumpkin with Onions and Fenugreek
## *Kaddoo Ki Sabzi*

Cooked in the Uttar Pradesh style, this dish is a specialty of my mother-in-law. She often serves it with a dal and Shallow-Fried Wheat Bread. Choose ripe pumpkins for this recipe; their natural sweetness adds flavor to the dish.

**1 pumpkin (about 2 1/2 pounds)**
**2 medium onions**
**2 large cloves garlic**
**3 tablespoons vegetable oil**
**Pinch crushed asafoetida (optional)**
**1/2 teaspoon fenugreek seeds**
**1 teaspoon ground coriander seeds**
**1/2 teaspoon ground turmeric**
**Salt, to taste**
**1/4 teaspoon cayenne pepper**
**1/2 teaspoon sugar**
**2 tablespoons lemon juice**

Halve the pumpkin and scrape away the seeds and fiber. Slice it, then cut it into 1-inch pieces. Peel the pieces and set aside.

Slice the onions into thin half rounds. Finely chop the garlic. In a large heavy-bottomed skillet over medium heat, warm the oil. Add the asafoetida (if used) and fenugreek seeds. When the spices darken (1 to 2 seconds), add the chopped garlic. Cook for 1 minute, then add the sliced onions and saute until browned (12 to 15 minutes). Add the ground coriander seeds, turmeric, salt, cayenne, and sugar; cook for 1 minute. Add the pumpkin pieces and toss to mix. Cover, reduce the heat to low, and cook until the pumpkin is tender (20 to 25 minutes). Uncover, increase the heat to high, and boil away any remaining liquid. Mix in the lemon juice and serve.

Yield: Serves 4 with other dishes.

# Spinach with Cottage Cheese

## *Saag Paneer*

This extremely popular dish from North India can also be made with cooked diced potatoes instead of cottage cheese. For a richer dish, the potatoes may be deep-fried. I sometimes replace the cottage cheese with button mushrooms and serve it with Chicken in Sour Cream and Nuts and Shallow-Fried Wheat Bread.

1 recipe homemade cottage cheese
Vegetable oil, for deep-frying
2 medium onions
1/2-inch piece fresh ginger
4 cloves garlic
4 tablespoons vegetable oil
1/2 teaspoon cumin seeds
1 bay leaf
1-inch stick cinnamon
2 whole cloves
4 tablespoons sour cream or plain yogurt
20 ounces (2 packets) frozen chopped spinach,
   cooked and drained
1/2 cup water
Salt, to taste
1/4 teaspoon cayenne pepper
1/4 cup whipping cream

Dice the cottage cheese into 3/4-inch cubes. Warm the oil for deep-frying over medium heat. Gently fry the cottage cheese cubes until lightly browned on all sides. Drain on paper towels and set aside. In the container of a blender or food processor, mince the onions, ginger, and garlic together.

In a large heavy-bottomed skillet over medium heat, warm the 4 tablespoons oil. Add the cumin, bay leaf, cinnamon, and cloves. When the spices darken (1 to 2 seconds), add the minced onion mixture. Reduce the heat to low and saute until the onions are golden brown (10 to 12 minutes), stirring occasionally. Add the sour cream and mix well. Place the spinach and the water in the container of a blender and blend to a smooth puree. Add to the onion mixture. Add the salt, cayenne, and cottage cheese cubes and toss gently with the spinach. Cover and cook for 5 minutes. Pour in the whipping cream and mix lightly. Heat through and serve.

Yield: Serves 4 with other dishes.

# Spinach with Chickpeas
## *Saag Chole*

This tasty, nutritious dish goes as well with French bread as with an Indian meal. It can be topped with grated cheese and baked in the oven. Diced potatoes could be used in place of the chickpeas for a different flavor. Serve with Chicken Curry and an Indian bread.

**2 medium onions**
**1/2-inch piece fresh ginger**
**2 cloves garlic**
**3 tablespoons vegetable oil**
**1/2 teaspoon cumin seeds**
**2 medium tomatoes, chopped coarsely**
**1/2 teaspoon ground coriander seeds**
**1/4 teaspoon ground turmeric**
**Salt, to taste**
**1/4 teaspoon cayenne pepper**
**20 ounces (2 packets) frozen chopped spinach, thawed and drained**
**1 1/2 cups cooked, drained chickpeas**
**1 teaspoon *garam masala***
**1 tablespoon lemon juice**

Slice the onions into thin half rounds. Grate the ginger and garlic. In a large heavy-bottomed skillet over medium heat, warm the oil. Add the cumin. When it darkens (1 to 2 seconds), add the grated ginger and garlic. Cook for 1 minute, then add the sliced onions and saute until lightly browned (about 8 minutes). Add the tomatoes and cook until soft (about 5 minutes). Add the coriander, turmeric, salt, and cayenne. Mix well, then add the spinach. Mix again, cover, reduce the heat to medium-low, and cook for 25 minutes, stirring occasionally. Mix in the chickpeas and cook for 5 more minutes. Add the *garam masala* and lemon juice, and serve hot.

Yield: Serves 4 with other dishes.

# Tomatoes with Chickpeas
## *Chole Bhare Tamatar*

This is an ideal dish to make when you are rushed for time. Served cold and unbaked, the tomatoes make a delicious salad.

**8 medium stuffing tomatoes (2 pounds total)**
**3/4 teaspoon ground coriander seeds**
**1/2 teaspoon ground cumin seeds**
**1/4 teaspoon ground roasted cumin seeds**
**1/2 teaspoon *garam masala***
**Salt, to taste**
**1/4 teaspoon cayenne pepper**
**2 cups cooked chickpeas, drained**
**2 tablespoons vegetable oil, for tomatoes**

With a sharp knife cut off a small portion of the top of each tomato; scoop out the pulp and reserve it. Save the caps. Lightly salt the inside of each tomato shell and arrange them upside down on a plate to drain. Mix half the tomato pulp and all the spices with the chickpeas, and mash coarsely. Stuff the tomatoes with this mixture and replace their caps. Preheat the oven to 350°F. Lightly oil the surface of each tomato and place it in a greased baking dish. Bake uncovered for 25 minutes. Serve hot.

Yield: Serves 4 with other dishes.

# Tomatoes with Mung Beans

### Moong Bhare Tamatar

The pulp scooped out of the tomatoes may be used in place of water for making chapati dough, rice, sauces, or soups. This dish goes well with Meatballs with Mint in Onion-Yogurt Sauce and Shallow-Fried Wheat Bread.

1/2 cup *dhuli moong dal* (hulled, split mung beans)
1 cup water
1 medium onion
1/4-inch piece fresh ginger
2 tablespoons vegetable oil
Pinch crushed asafoetida (optional)
1/2 teaspoon cumin seeds
Salt, to taste
1/4 teaspoon cayenne pepper
1/4 teaspoon ground turmeric
1/2 teaspoon *garam masala*
8 large stuffing tomatoes
2 tablespoons vegetable oil, for tomatoes

Wash the mung beans, place them and the water in a medium heavy-bottomed saucepan, and soak for 30 minutes. Meanwhile, chop the onion finely and grate the ginger. In a small heavy-bottomed skillet over medium heat, warm the oil. Add the asafoetida (if used) and cumin. When the spices darken (1 to 2 seconds), add the grated ginger. Cook for 1 minute, then add the chopped onion and saute over medium heat for 7 minutes. Transfer to a small bowl and set aside.

Add the salt, cayenne, and turmeric to the soaked mung beans. Bring to a boil over high heat, then cover, reduce the heat to medium, and cook for 10 minutes. Remove from the heat and add the reserved onion mixture and *garam masala*; mix gently so that the mung beans do not become mushy.

Cut off a small portion of the tops of the tomatoes and scoop out the pulp. Lightly salt the inside of each tomato shell and arrange them upside down on a plate to drain for a few minutes. Preheat the oven to 350°F. Stuff the tomatoes with the mung bean filling and lightly oil their surface. Place them in a greased baking dish and bake uncovered for 25 minutes. Serve hot.

Yield: Serves 4 with other dishes.

# Tomatoes with Cottage Cheese

## *Paneer Bhare Tamatar*

These stuffed tomatoes are a delicacy from the state of Uttar Pradesh. They are usually shallow-fried in oil, but I find baking an easier and healthier alternative. They could be served with Meatballs with Mint in Onion-Yogurt Sauce.

**8 medium stuffing tomatoes (2 pounds total)**
**Salt, to taste**
**2 medium onions**
**1/2-inch piece fresh ginger**
**2 tablespoons vegetable oil**
**1/2 teaspoon cumin seeds**
**1 cup crumbled homemade cottage cheese**
**  (page 00)**
**1 cup peas (fresh or frozen)**
**1/4 teaspoon cayenne pepper**
**1/2 teaspoon *garam masala***
**1/2 teaspoon ground coriander seeds**
**2 tablespoons vegetable oil, for tomatoes**

Cut off 1/4 inch of the tops of the tomatoes. Carefully scoop out the pulp. Dust the inside of the shells lightly with salt and arrange them upside down on a plate to drain. Reserve the pulp for another use. Chop the onions finely. Grate the ginger. In a large heavy-bottomed skillet over medium heat, warm the oil. Add the cumin. When it darkens (1 to 2 seconds), add the grated ginger. Cook for 1 minute, then add the chopped onions and saute until lightly browned (about 7 minutes). Add the cottage cheese, peas, cayenne, *garam masala*, and coriander, and cook for 5 minutes.

Preheat the oven to 350°F. Stuff the tomatoes with the cottage cheese mixture. Lightly coat each tomato with vegetable oil and place in a greased ovenproof dish. Bake uncovered for 20 to 25 minutes. Serve hot.

Yield: Serves 4 with other dishes.

# Tomatoes and Potatoes in Sweet-and-Sour Sauce

## *Hare Tamatar Aur Alu Ki Sabzi*

This is one of the few sweet-and-sour dishes of Indian cuisine. Tart green tomatoes are cooked with potatoes in a lightly sweetened sauce aromatized with whole spices. It is a simple yet delicious dish that could be served with Chicken with Mustard and Pan-Broiled Wheat Bread.

**4 medium potatoes**
**1/2-inch piece fresh ginger**
**1 green chilli (optional)**
**2 tablespoons vegetable oil**
**1/4 teaspoon fenugreek seeds**
**1/4 teaspoon *kalonji* (onion seeds)**
**1/4 teaspoon fennel seeds**
**1/4 teaspoon cumin seeds**
**1/4 teaspoon black mustard seeds**
**4 medium green tomatoes, chopped coarsely**
**Salt, to taste**
**1/2 teaspoon ground turmeric**
**1/2 cup water**
**2 tablespoons sugar**

Cook the potatoes until tender. Peel and dice into 3/4-inch pieces; set aside. Grate the ginger and chop the chilli. In a large heavy-bottomed skillet over medium heat, warm oil. Add the fenugreek, onion seeds, fennel, cumin, and mustard seeds. When the spices puff up and darken, add the grated ginger. Cook for 1 minute, then add the tomatoes, salt, turmeric, and the water. Cover, reduce the heat to low, and cook for 12 to 15 minutes. Add the reserved potatoes and sugar. Mix well and cook for 5 to 7 minutes. Serve hot.

Yield: Serves 4 with other dishes.

# Cottage Cheese in Tomato-Cashew Sauce

## *Malai Kofte*

Diwali, one of the biggest Hindu festivals in India, is celebrated with great gusto all over the country. It marks the return of the God Rama after 14 years of exile in the forest. Tiny oil lamps are lit in welcome in every corner of the house, inside as well as out, and firecrackers burst merrily well into the early hours of the morning. Friends and relatives visit each other carrying boxes of sweets and nuts; dinner is a festive occasion. These *kofte* in their rich sauce would be suitable for just such a meal. Serve them with a *pullao* (spiced rice) of your choice and Baked Chicken.

1 medium cooked potato
1 cup crumbled homemade cottage cheese
1/4 teaspoon salt
2 tablespoons all-purpose flour
Vegetable oil, for deep-frying
1/2-inch piece fresh ginger
1 clove garlic
1/4 cup broken cashew nut pieces
1 3/4 cups fresh tomato puree
1/4 teaspoon cayenne pepper
Salt, to taste
1/2 teaspoon ground turmeric
1/2 teaspoon ground cumin seeds
1/2 teaspoon ground coriander seeds
1/2 teaspoon *garam masala*
1/2 teaspoon sugar

Peel and mash the potato. Add the cottage cheese, salt, and flour and knead well with the heel of your hand for about 5 minutes. Shape the mixture into balls about 1 1/2 inches in diameter, making sure there are no cracks on the surface. Cover the balls with plastic wrap and refrigerate for 30 minutes. If you wish to omit this step, you may proceed directly to deep-frying them.

Warm the oil for deep-frying over medium-low heat and fry the balls until they are golden brown on all sides. Drain on paper towels and set aside.

Grate the ginger and garlic. In a large heavy-bottomed skillet over low heat, dry-roast the cashews until they are brown speckled; let cool, then grind finely. To the same skillet over low heat, add the tomato puree, grated ginger and garlic, cayenne, salt, turmeric, cumin, coriander, *garam masala*, sugar, and ground cashews. Cook for 8 to 10 minutes. Arrange the fried cottage cheese balls in a deep dish and pour the sauce over them just before serving.

Yield: Serves 4 with other dishes.

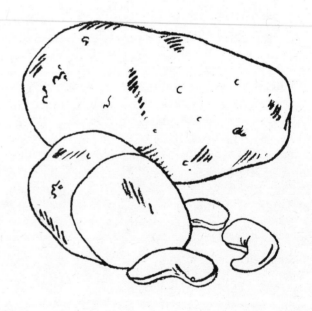

# Zucchini with Dumplings

## *Lauki Pakodi*

This simple, easy-to-prepare dish is lightly seasoned with whole spices. The dumplings soak up the sauce and become spongy and delicious. You could, if you wish, make the zucchini without the dumplings, but I think they add character to the dish.

2 medium zucchini
1 tablespoon vegetable oil
Pinch crushed asafoetida (optional)
1/4 teaspoon cumin seeds
1/2 teaspoon fennel seeds
1/4 teaspoon *kalonji* (onion seeds)
1/4 teaspoon fenugreek seeds
1/4 teaspoon black mustard seeds
1 bay leaf
1/2 teaspoon ground turmeric
Salt, to taste
1/4 teaspoon cayenne pepper
1/4 cup water
2 tablespoons lemon juice

*Dumplings*

1/2 cup chickpea flour
7 tablespoons
Vegetable oil, for deep-frying

Peel and dice the zucchini into 1-inch pieces. In a large heavy-bottomed skillet over medium heat, warm the oil. Add the asafoetida (if used), cumin, fennel, onion seeds, fenugreek, mustard seeds, and bay leaf. When the spices darken (1 to 2 seconds), add the zucchini pieces, tumeric, salt, and cayenne. Add the 1/4 cup water, cover, reduce the heat to low, and cook until the zucchini is tender (about 10 minutes).

To prepare the dumplings, make a smooth batter with the chickpea flour and the 7 tablespoons water. Heat the oil for deep-frying over medium-high heat. With a tablespoon, drop enough batter in to make plump, round dumplings. Reduce the heat to medium and fry until the dumplings are golden brown on all sides.

Drain the dumplings on paper towels and add them to the zucchini mixture along with the lemon juice. Mix very gently, cover, and cook over low heat for 5 minutes. Serve hot.

Yield: Serves 4 with other dishes.

# Zucchini Dumplings in Onion-Tomato Sauce

## *Lauki Ke Kofte*

You can also serve these dumplings in Spinach with Cottage Cheese. Just omit the cottage cheese from that recipe, add the dumplings, and you have a new dish for the vegetarians in your family.

2 large zucchini (about 2 pounds)
1 teaspoon salt
1/3 cup plus 1 tablespoon chickpea flour
Vegetable oil, for deep-frying
2 medium onions
2 cloves garlic
1/2-inch piece fresh ginger
3 tablespoons vegetable oil
1/2 teaspoon cumin seeds
2 medium tomatoes, chopped coarsely
1/2 teaspoon ground turmeric
Salt, to taste
1/4 teaspoon cayenne pepper
1/4 teaspoon freshly ground black pepper
1/2 teaspoon ground coriander seeds
1/2 teaspoon *garam masala*
1 tablespoon lemon juice

Peel and grate the zucchini. Squeeze out all the excess juice with your hands and reserve the juice. Mix the salt and chickpea flour into the grated zucchini. Warm the oil for deep-frying over medium-high heat. Make balls 1 to 1 1/2 inches in diameter from the zucchini mixture and drop them gently into the hot oil. Reduce the heat to medium-low and fry until golden brown on all sides. Drain on paper towels and keep warm.

In the container of a food processor or blender, mince the onions, garlic, and ginger together. In a large heavy-bottomed skillet over medium heat, warm the 3 tablespoons oil. Add the cumin. When it darkens (1 to 2 seconds), add the minced onion mixture. Reduce the heat to medium-low and saute until the onions are browned (20 to 25 minutes). Add the tomatoes, turmeric, salt, cayenne, black pepper, coriander, and *garam masala*. Cook until the tomatoes are soft (5 to 7 minutes). Measure out the juice saved from squeezing the grated zucchini and add enough water to make 1 cup. Add to the sauce and simmer for 5 to 7 minutes. Add the zucchini dumplings and lemon juice. Serve hot.

Yield: Serves 4 with other dishes.

# Zucchini with Onions

## *Pyaz Lauki*

6 baby zucchini, ends removed
2 medium onions
1/2-inch piece fresh ginger
2 tablespoons vegetable oil
1/2 teaspoon fenugreek seeds
1/2 teaspoon ground turmeric
Salt, to taste
1/4 teaspoon cayenne pepper
Sour cream (optional)

Scrape each zucchini lightly with a knife, then wash and quarter lengthwise. Set aside. Peel and slice the onions into thin half rounds. Grate the ginger. In a large heavy-bottomed skillet over medium heat, warm the oil. Add the fenugreek. When it darkens (1 to 2 seconds), add the grated ginger. Cook for 1 minute, then add the sliced onions and saute until browned (5 to 7 minutes).

Add the turmeric, salt, cayenne, and zucchini fingers and stir to mix. Cover, reduce the heat to low, and cook until the zucchini is tender (20 to 25 minutes). Serve with a dollop of sour cream, if desired.

Yield: Serves 4 with other dishes.

# Raitas & Salads

An Indian meal is a well thought-out balance of textures and flavors in which soft foods are matched with crunchy ones and cooling dishes offset the hot and spicy ones. Raitas and salads are important components of the meal, since they not only soothe and refresh the palate, but also provide the zest and crunch of fresh vegetables and fruits.

The kind of salads served in an Indian meal are very different from those served in a Western one. For instance, instead of salad dressings, we use salt and lemon juice. Sometimes a little black pepper or ground roasted cumin seeds are also sprinkled on top. Most salads consist of just one basic ingredient, such as cucumber wedges served with ground roasted cumin seeds, or tomato rounds with a dash of freshly ground black pepper. A more elaborate salad may consist of two or three basic ingredients, such as onion, cucumbers, and tomatoes tossed together, or different fruits chopped and tossed with sugar and lemon juice. Rarely would a salad form the bulk of the meal. Its main role is as a side dish designed to cool the palate. It can be served chilled or at room temperature.

Raitas are the closest thing we have to a salad served with dressing. Raitas are always yogurt based. Depending on the region they come from, other ingredients are added, which makes raitas very versatile. Vegetables such as cucumber, zucchini, onions, or tomatoes, and herbs such as fresh coriander or mint are added to the raita. Spices such as ground roasted cumin seeds and black salt or mustard seed-infused oil are also added for aroma and flavor. Or lentil or chickpea dumplings can be added instead. Raitas can also be flavored with cardamom and served sweet with fruits and nuts.

# Salad of Mixed Vegetables
## *Sabzi Ka Salat*

This is a good salad to serve when the other dishes on the menu are hot and spicy.

**1 small cucumber**
**1 small onion**
**2 medium tomatoes**
**1 tablespoon chopped fresh coriander leaves**
**Salt, to taste**
**1 tablespoon lemon juice**

Peel the cucumber and onion and chop finely. Finely dice the tomatoes. Transfer to a bowl and toss with the coriander, salt, and lemon juice. Serve chilled or at room temperature.

Yield: Serves 4 with other dishes.

# Cucumber with Cumin
## *Kheere Ka Salat*

This is a simple, mildly spiced salad that brings a fresh, crisp crunch to a meal.

**1 medium cucumber**
**Salt, to taste**
**1/2 teaspoon ground roasted cumin seeds**
**2 tablespoons lemon juice**

Peel and quarter the cucumber, then cut it into 1-inch-long wedges, or slice it into rounds if you prefer. Arrange on a platter and sprinkle evenly with the salt, cumin, and lemon juice. Serve chilled or at room temperature.

Yield: Serves 4 with other dishes.

# Onion and Cucumber Salad

## *Kheere Pyaz Ka Salat*

In this salad, which is most often served at parties, thin slices of tomato can also be alternated with the onion and cucumber, giving the dish a striking contrast of colors, flavors, and textures.

**2 medium onions**
**1 medium cucumber**
**3 tablespoons finely chopped fresh coriander**
**  leaves**
**Salt, to taste**
**1/2 teaspoon ground roasted cumin seeds**
**2 tablespoons lemon juice**

Peel the onions and cucumber and slice into thin rounds. Arrange alternate slices of onion and cucumber on a serving platter. Spread the coriander leaves evenly over top, then sprinkle evenly with the salt, cumin, and lemon juice. Serve chilled or at room temperature.

Yield: Serves 4 with other dishes.

# Onion Rings in Vinegar

## *Pyaz Sirkewali*

At *dhabas*, the roadside eateries of northern India, onion rings marinated in vinegar are placed on the table for people to munch on while they peruse the menu and debate the merits of tandoori chicken versus kebabs. Onion rings or pickled onions are traditionally served with all barbecued preparations.

**2 medium onions**
**1/4 teaspoon salt**
**3 tablespoons distilled white vinegar**

Peel and slice the onions into thin rounds. Separate the rings and arrange on a serving dish. Sprinkle evenly with the salt, then pour the vinegar evenly over all the slices. Cover the onions and let them marinate at room temperature for at least 30 minutes before you intend to serve them. Toss them occasionally to make sure they marinate thoroughly. Serve chilled or at room temperature.

Yield: Serves 4 with other dishes.

# Daikon Salad

## *Mooli Ka Salat*

If you have seen daikon—a long, thick white radish—at the supermarket but have never known what to do with it, here is a simple recipe to start with. It is slightly sharp to the taste and goes well with spiced rice, such as *biryanis* or *pullaos*. You can also add some grated cucumber and carrots and chopped fresh coriander to this dish to counteract some of the sharpness of the radish.

**Medium piece daikon (about 7 inches long)**
**Salt, to taste**
**2 tablespoons lemon juice**

Scrape the daikon, wash, and grate in a food processor or with a hand grater. Transfer to a serving dish and mix in the salt and lemon juice. Serve chilled or at room temperature.

Yield: Serves 4 with other dishes.

# Tomato Salad
## *Tamatar Ka Salat*

Slices of juicy tomato with just a hint of roasted cumin seeds are a wonderful addition to any meal.

3 medium tomatoes
Salt, to taste
Lemon juice, to taste
1/2 teaspoon ground roasted cumin seeds
1/2 teaspoon freshly ground black pepper
1 tablespoon chopped fresh coriander leaves
   (optional), for garnish

Slice the tomatoes into thin rounds and arrange on a serving dish. Sprinkle evenly with the salt, lemon juice, cumin, and pepper, then garnish with coriander leaves (if used). Serve chilled or at room temperature.

Yield: Serves 4 with other dishes.

# Sweet-and-Sour Tomato Salad
## *Khatta Meetha Salat*

This is my mother's version of an unusual sweet-and-sour salad from the state of Uttar Pradesh. You could also make it without the green onions.

2 medium tomatoes
4 green onions
1/4-inch piece fresh ginger
1 green chilli (deseeded if desired)
2 tablespoons chopped fresh coriander leaves
1/2 teaspoon sugar
Pinch salt
1 tablespoon lemon juice

Chop the tomatoes coarsely. Chop the green onions finely, including 2 inches of the green part. Peel and chop the ginger very finely. Chop the green chilli finely. In a large bowl toss all the ingredients together; let stand for 15 minutes in the refrigerator for the flavors to blend before serving.

Yield: Serves 4 with other dishes.

# Carrot Salad
## *Gajar Nu Salat*

This salad from Gujarat is an unusual and delicious way to serve carrots.

3/4 pound carrots
2 tablespoons vegetable oil
1 teaspoon black mustard seeds
Salt, to taste
Pinch sugar
2 tablespoons lemon juice

Trim, scrape, and grate the carrots. In a medium size, heavy-bottomed skillet over high heat, warm the oil. Add the mustard seeds; as soon as they begin to splutter, add the grated carrots, salt, and sugar. Stir for 1 minute, then remove from the heat. Let cool to room temperature and mix in the lemon juice. Serve chilled or at room temperature.

Yield: Serves 4 with other dishes.

# Chickpea and Herb Salad
## *Chola Chaat*

On hot summer days, I serve this salad with a *lassi* (yogurt drink) for a light and refreshing meal. This salad is substantial enough to double as a side dish for dinner, too.

1/4 cup fresh mint leaves
1/4 cup fresh coriander leaves and tender upper
    stems
1/4-inch piece fresh ginger
1 green chilli (optional)
1 1/2 tablespoons lemon juice
4 green onions
1 medium cooked potato
1 1/2 cups cooked chickpeas, drained
Salt, to taste
1/4 teaspoon cayenne pepper
1/2 teaspoon ground roasted cumin seeds
1/4 teaspoon *kala namak* (black salt)

In the container of a blender or food processor, mince together into a paste the mint, coriander, ginger, chilli, and lemon juice; set aside. Finely chop the green onions, including 2 inches of the green part. Peel and dice the potato into 1/2-inch or smaller cubes.

In a large bowl combine the chickpeas, chopped green onions, and diced potato. Add the salt, cayenne, cumin, and kala namak (if used). Toss well, then mix in the minced coriander paste and toss to thoroughly coat the chickpeas and potatoes. Serve chilled or at room temperature.

Yield: Serves 4 with other dishes.

# Cucumber in Yogurt
## *Kheere Ka Raita*

The addition of chopped walnuts or roasted peanuts gives this raita a pleasant crunch.

1 cup plain yogurt
1/4 cup water
Salt, to taste
1/4 teaspoon cayenne pepper
1/4 teaspoon ground roasted cumin seeds
1/4 teaspoon *kala namak* (black salt)
1 medium cucumber

Place the yogurt in a large bowl and beat with a spoon until smooth. Add the water, salt, cayenne, cumin, and kala namak. Peel and grate the cucumber and add to the beaten yogurt. Mix well and serve chilled or at room temperature.

Yield: Serves 4 with other dishes.

# Cucumber in Lightly Spiced Yogurt

## *Kheera Pachadi*

This raita is popular in northern as well as southern India, although its spicing shows interesting regional variations. Northerners use ground roasted cumin seeds and black salt to pep up their raitas; this recipe from Kerala in southern India calls for mustard seeds and curry leaves.

**1 medium cucumber**
**1 cup plain yogurt**
**1/4 cup water**
**Salt, to taste**
**1 tablespoon vegetable oil**
**1/2 teaspoon black mustard seeds**
**4 or 5 dried curry leaves**

Peel and grate the cucumber. Place the yogurt in a large bowl and beat with a spoon until smooth. Add the water, salt, and grated cucumber.

In a small heavy-bottomed skillet over medium heat, warm the oil. Add the mustard seeds and curry leaves and cook until the mustard seeds splutter. Pour the spiced oil over the yogurt mixture, stir gently, and serve chilled or at room temperature.

Yield: Serves 4 with other dishes.

# Cucumber and Mint in Yogurt

## *Kheere Podhine Ka Raita*

In northern India, this raita is featured in many meals. The crunchy cucumber and mint freshen the palate, and the yogurt tempers the heat of the spices in the other dishes.

**1 cup plain yogurt**
**Salt, to taste**
**1/4 teaspoon cayenne pepper**
**1/4 teaspoon ground roasted cumin seeds**
**1/4 teaspoon *kala namak* (black salt)**
**1 medium cucumber**
**3/4 cup loosely packed fresh mint leaves**
**1/2 cup water**

Place the yogurt in a large bowl and beat with a spoon until smooth. Add the salt, cayenne, cumin, and kala namak. Peel and grate the cucumber and add to the yogurt mixture.

In the container of a blender or food processor, blend the mint and the water to a smooth puree. Add to the cucumber-yogurt mixture. Serve chilled or at room temperature.

Yield: Serves 4 with other dishes.

# Yogurt with Mint

## *Podhine Ka Raita*

We often have this raita—my father's favorite—with lunch on a hot summer day. I also like to eat it over rice.

**1 cup plain yogurt**
**3/4 cup loosely packed fresh mint leaves**
**1/2 cup water**
**Salt, to taste**
**1/4 teaspoon *kala namak* (black salt)**
**1/2 teaspoon ground roasted cumin seeds**

Place the yogurt in a large bowl and beat well with a spoon. In the container of a blender, mince the mint leaves along with 1/4 cup of the water until smooth. Add to the yogurt along with the salt, kala namak, cumin, and the remaining 1/4 cup water. Mix well and serve chilled or at room temperature.

Yield: Serves 4 with other dishes.

# Yogurt with Potatoes and Mint

## *Podhine Alu Ka Raita*

This minty creation is a refreshing side dish when spicy entrees are on the menu.

**1 cup plain yogurt**
**Salt, to taste**
**1/4 teaspoon ground roasted cumin seeds**
**1/4 teaspoon *kala namak* (black salt)**
**1 large cooked potato**
**1 cup loosely packed fresh mint leaves**
**1/2 cup water**

Place the yogurt in a large bowl and beat with a spoon until smooth. Mix in the salt, cumin, and kala namak. Peel the potato, mash it coarsely, and mix it into the yogurt.

In the container of a food processor or blender, grind the mint leaves and the water to a smooth paste. Add to the yogurt mixture, stir to combine, and serve chilled or at room temperature.

Yield: Serves 4 with other dishes.

# Bananas in Cardamom-Flavored Yogurt

## *Kele Ka Raita*

Peeled diced apples or pineapple chunks may be substituted for the bananas.

**2 ripe bananas**
**1 cup plain yogurt**
**2 tablespoons sugar**
**4 cardamom pods**

Peel the bananas and slice thinly. Place the yogurt in a large bowl and beat with a spoon until smooth. Mix in the sugar. Remove the seeds from the cardamom pods and grind the seeds. Add to the yogurt mixture along with the bananas. Stir to mix and serve chilled or at room temperature.

Yield: Serves 4 with other dishes.

# Vegetables in Yogurt

## *Sabzi Ka Raita*

Raitas are refreshingly different salads. The cool, lightly spiced yogurt base makes a healthy dressing that can be varied in a number of ways to create new flavors.

**1 medium cucumber**
**1 medium tomato**
**1 small onion**
**1 small cooked potato**
**1 cup plain yogurt**
**1/2 cup water**
**1/2 teaspoon ground roasted cumin seeds**
**Salt, to taste**
**2 tablespoons chopped mint leaves (optional)**

Peel the cucumber and chop into 1/4-inch pieces. Chop the tomato into 1/4-inch pieces. Chop the onion finely. Peel and dice the potato into 1/4-inch cubes.

Place the yogurt in a large bowl and beat well with a spoon. Add the water, cumin, and salt. Gently stir in the chopped vegetables and mint (if used), and serve chilled or at room temperature.

Yield: Serves 4 with other dishes.

# Lentil Dumplings in Yogurt
## *Pakodi Ka Raita*

For a delicious appetizer, add some salt, cayenne, cumin seed, and chopped onions to the dumpling batter and serve these morsels without the yogurt. You can also turn them into a side dish for dinner by serving them in any sauce of your choice instead of in the spiced yogurt. Omit soaking the dumplings in water if you follow the above suggestions.

1/2 cup *dhuli urad dal* (black gram beans, split and hulled)
Vegetable oil, for deep-frying
1 cup plain yogurt
1/2 cup water
Salt, to taste
1/4 teaspoon cayenne pepper
1/4 teaspoon *kala namak* (black salt)
1/2 teaspoon ground roasted cumin seeds

Soak the beans in enough water to cover for at least 3 hours; drain. In the container of a blender or food processor, grind the soaked beans to a fine paste, adding a sprinkling of water if necessary.

Warm the oil for deep-frying over medium heat. Fill a large pot with water and place nearby. Wetting your hands lightly, shape walnut-sized balls from the bean paste and drop them gently into the hot oil. Fry until golden, drain on paper towels, and transfer to pot of water to soak.

Place the yogurt in a small bowl and beat with a spoon until smooth. Add the water, salt, cayenne, kala namak, and cumin; mix well. Remove the dumplings from the water, squeeze them lightly, and place them in a large bowl. Pour the yogurt over them. Serve chilled or at room temperature.

Yield: Serves 4 with other dishes.

# Mixed Vegetables in Lightly Spiced Yogurt
## *Pachadi*

The distinctive spicing of mustard seeds and curry leaves makes this cooling, crunchy raita from South India a good accompaniment to the fiery southern dishes.

1 cup plain yogurt
Salt, to taste
1/4 teaspoon cayenne pepper
1/4 cup water
1 medium cucumber
1 small onion
1 small tomato
1 tablespoon vegetable oil
1/2 teaspoon black mustard seeds
4 or 5 dried curry leaves

Place the yogurt in a large bowl and beat with a spoon until smooth. Stir in the salt, cayenne, and the water. Peel the cucumber and onion and chop into very small pieces. Finely chop the tomato. Add these to the yogurt.

In a small heavy-bottomed skillet over medium heat, warm the oil. Add the mustard seeds and curry leaves and cook until the seeds splutter. Remove from the heat and pour the spiced oil over the yogurt mixture, stir gently, and serve chilled or at room temperature.

Yield: Serves 4 with other dishes.

# Zucchini in Yogurt
## *Lauki Ka Raita*

An unusual combination of spices makes this raita refreshingly different. It is a good accompaniment to bland rice pullaos.

**1 medium zucchini**
**1 cup plain yogurt**
**1 1/4 cups water**
**Salt, to taste**
**1/4 teaspoon sugar**
**1/4 teaspoon cayenne pepper**
**1 tablespoon vegetable oil**
**1 cardamom pod**
**10 black peppercorns**
**1/2 teaspoon cumin seeds**
**1/4 teaspoon black mustard seeds**
**Pinch crushed asafoetida (optional)**

Peel and grate the zucchini. Place it in a pan with 1 cup of the water and bring to a boil over high heat. Cook for 5 minutes. Drain and let cool, then squeeze out the excess water with your hands.

Place the yogurt in a large bowl and beat with a spoon until smooth. Mix in the remaining 1/4 cup water, salt, sugar, and cayenne.

In a small heavy-bottomed skillet over medium heat, warm the oil. Add the cardamom, black peppercorns, cumin seeds, mustard seeds, and asafoetida (if used). Cook until the spices darken (1 to 2 seconds), then remove from the heat and grind the spices finely into a paste.

Stir the paste into the yogurt mixture. Add the cooled zucchini and stir gently with a fork to separate the strands. Serve chilled or at room temperature.

Yield: Serves 4 with other dishes.

Rice

In the South, rice is the staple food and is eaten in some form at every meal. Breakfast may consist of *dosas*, crepes made from fermented rice flour and lentils; lunch may be a simple dish of leftover rice mixed with yogurt and spices; and dinner may center around a spicy vegetable or meat *pullao*. Though rice is not eaten at every meal in the North, it is nonetheless very popular and is cooked in many different ways. It may be eaten plain-boiled as an accompaniment to the main dish; combined with lentils or with meat, poultry, or seafood to form *biryanis* and *pullaos*; and may also be made into a dessert, snacks, pappadams, dumplings, and crepes.

There are two principal varieties of rice eaten in India: long grain and basmati. The long-grain variety is for daily use and is often cooked plain. Basmati rice, a fragrant grain and the more expensive of the two, is reserved for festive occasions. *Biryanis* and *pullaos* are created from basmati rice, which adds its own special aroma to the flavor of these dishes.

# Long-Grain Rice
## *Saaday Chaval*

Rice is a good accompaniment to many dishes. Leftover rice can be used in other dishes: It is delicious mashed with cooked potatoes, formed into dumplings, and deep-fried. The dumplings can later be served in any sauce of your choice. Mashed rice can also be mixed into the dough for Pan-Broiled Wheat Bread.

**1 cup long-grain rice**
**1 1/2 cups water**
**1 teaspoon butter**
**Pinch salt**

Wash the rice well under running water. Place it in a heavy-bottomed saucepan along with the water, butter, and salt. Cover and bring to a boil over high heat, then reduce the heat to very low and cook for 20 minutes without uncovering the pan.

Turn off the heat and let the pan stand covered on the burner for 5 minutes. Then uncover, fluff up the rice gently with a fork, and serve.

Yield: Serves 4 with other dishes.

# Rice with Peas
## *Matar Pullao*

Popular at special dinners, Matar Pullao is a perfect choice because of its delicate spicing, which doesn't interfere with the flavors of the main dishes.

**1 cup basmati rice**
**1 cup water**
**1 medium onion**
**2 tablespoons vegetable oil**
**1/2 teaspoon cumin seeds**
**1/2-inch stick cinnamon**
**2 cloves**
**1 cardamom pod**
**1 bay leaf**
**Salt, to taste**
**1 cup peas, fresh or frozen**

Wash the rice under running water, then let it soak in the 1 cup water. Slice the onion into thin half rounds.

In a large heavy-bottomed saucepan over medium heat, warm the oil. Add the cumin, cinnamon, cloves, cardamom pod, and bay leaf. When the spices puff up and darken (1 to 2 seconds), add the sliced onions and saute until golden brown (about 12 minutes). Reduce the heat to low and add the rice and its soaking liquid, salt, and peas. Mix gently, cover, increase the heat to high, and bring to a boil. Then reduce the heat to very low and cook for 25 minutes without uncovering the pan.

Turn off the heat and let the pan stand covered on the burner for 5 minutes. Then uncover, fluff up the rice gently with a fork, and serve.

Yield: Serves 4 with other dishes.

# Mushroom Rice
## *Kumbhi Pullao*

In this dish the rice is lightly spiced so as not to overpower the delicate flavor of the mushrooms. You can serve Mushroom Rice with any dish needing a rice accompaniment.

**1 cup basmati rice**
**1 cup water**
**3/4 pound mushrooms**
**1 medium onion**
**2 tablespoons vegetable oil**
**1/2 teaspoon cumin seeds**
**1/2-inch stick cinnamon**
**1 bay leaf**
**2 cloves**
**10 black peppercorns**
**2 cardamom pods**
**Salt, to taste**

Wash the rice under running water, then let it soak in the 1 cup water. Wipe the mushrooms with a damp cloth and slice them thickly. Slice the onion into thin half rounds.

In a large heavy-bottomed saucepan over medium heat, warm the oil. Add the cumin, cinnamon, bay leaf, cloves, peppercorns, and cardamom pods. Cook until the spices darken (1 to 2 seconds), then add the sliced onions and saute until lightly browned (about 8 minutes). Add the sliced mushrooms and saute for another 5 to 6 minutes. Add the rice and its soaking water and salt, and stir gently. Cover, increase the heat to high, and bring to a boil. Then reduce the heat to very low and cook for 25 minutes without uncovering the pan.

Turn off the heat and let the pan stand covered on the burner for 5 to 7 minutes. Then uncover, fluff up the rice gently with a fork, and serve.

Yield: Serves 4 with other dishes.

# Carrot Rice
## *Gajar Ka Pullao*

Carrots add a mild sweetness to this pullao, which is lightly flavored with whole spices. The recipe was given to me by my sister-in-law Rachna, who entices her family to eat carrots this way.

**1 cup basmati rice**
**1 cup water**
**1 large onion**
**2 tablespoons vegetable oil**
**1 bay leaf**
**1/2 teaspoon cumin seeds**
**2 cloves**
**1 cardamom pod**
**1/2-inch stick cinnamon**
**1/2 teaspoon peppercorns**
**2 cups grated carrot**
**Salt, to taste**

Wash the rice under running water, then let soak in the 1 cup water. Slice the onion into thin half rounds.

In a large heavy-bottomed saucepan over medium heat, warm the oil. Add the bay leaf, cumin, cloves, cardamom pod, cinnamon, and peppercorns. Cook until the spices puff up and darken (1 to 2 seconds), then add the sliced onion and saute until browned (8 to 10 minutes). Add the carrot and saute for another 5 minutes. Add the rice and its soaking water and the salt. Stir gently, cover, increase the heat to high, and bring to a boil. Then reduce the heat to very low and cook for 25 minutes without uncovering the pan.

Turn off the heat and let the pan stand covered on the burner for 5 minutes. Then uncover, fluff up the rice gently, and serve.

Yield: Serves 4 with other dishes.

# Chicken and Rice Casserole
## *Kashmiri Pullao*

For the flavors of this pullao to be truly appreciated, it should be eaten without other main dishes. A simple raita would be an adequate accompaniment. Lamb can be used in place of the chicken.

**1 pound chicken breasts or thighs**
**1 cup basmati rice**
**1 1/2 cups water**
**3 tablespoons vegetable oil**
**1 cardamom pod**
**1 clove**
**1/2-inch stick cinnamon**
**1 bay leaf**
**1 teaspoon cumin seeds**
**Salt, to taste**
**1 teaspoon *garam masala***

Skin and debone the chicken and cut it into 1/2-inch pieces. Pat dry with a paper towel and set aside. Wash the rice under running water, then let it soak in the 1 1/2 cups water.

In a large heavy-bottomed saucepan over medium heat, warm the oil. Add the cardamom pod, clove, cinnamon, bay leaf, and cumin. Cook until the spices puff up and darken (1 to 2 seconds), then add the chicken pieces and cook for 5 minutes, stirring occasionally. Add the rice and its soaking liquid and the salt. Stir gently, cover, increase the heat to high, and bring to a boil. Then reduce the heat to very low and cook for 25 minutes without uncovering the pan.

Turn off the heat and let the pan stand covered on the burner for 5 minutes. Then uncover, gently mix in the *garam masala*, and serve.

Yield: Serves 4 with other dishes.

# Tomato-Rice Casserole
## *Tamatar Pullao*

1 cup basmati rice
1 cup water
3/4 pound ripe tomatoes
1 medium onion
3 tablespoons vegetable oil
1/2 teaspoon cumin seeds
1 bay leaf
2 cloves
1/2-inch stick cinnamon
1 cardamom pod
1 teaspoon peppercorns, coarsely crushed
1/2 cup peas, fresh or frozen
Salt, to taste
1/2 teaspoon ground turmeric

Wash the rice under running water, then let it soak in the 1 cup water. Puree the tomatoes in a food processor. Slice the onion in thin half rounds.

In a large heavy-bottomed saucepan over medium heat, warm 2 tablespoons of the oil. Add the sliced onion and saute until well browned (12 to 15 minutes). Separate the slices into rings and spread on paper towels to drain.

Warm the remaining 1 tablespoon oil in the pan. Add the cumin, bay leaf, cloves, cinnamon, and cardamom pod. When the spices puff up and darken (1 to 2 seconds), add the rice and its soaking water, tomato puree, pepper, peas, salt, and turmeric. Gently stir, cover, increase the heat to high, and bring to a boil. Then reduce the heat to very low and cook for 25 minutes.

Turn off the heat and let the pan stand covered on the burner for 5 minutes. Transfer the mixture to a serving dish and garnish with the sauteed onions. Serve hot.

Yield: Serves 4 with other dishes.

# Yogurt Rice
## *Thayir Sadam*

This extremely popular dish from South India doubles as a snack. Scores of office goers catching a quick bite for lunch at restaurants order this combination; little schoolchildren taking a break from unfathomable math dip into their lunch boxes containing refreshing yogurt rice to prepare them for the rigors of the remaining school day; and housewives faced with unexpected guests turn leftover rice into this perky dish.

2 medium onions
1/2-inch piece fresh ginger
2 cloves garlic
1 green chilli *or* 1/4 teaspoon cayenne pepper
2 tablespoons vegetable oil
1/2 teaspoon black mustard seeds
Pinch crushed asafoetida (optional)
8 to 10 dried curry leaves
Salt, to taste
4 cups cooked rice (basmati or long-grain)
1 cup plain yogurt, beaten with a spoon
1 tablespoon chopped fresh coriander leaves, for garnish (optional)

Chop the onions finely. Grate the ginger and garlic. Chop the chilli finely.

In a large heavy-bottomed skillet over medium heat, warm the oil. Add the mustard seeds and asafoetida (if used) and cook until the seeds splutter. Add the grated ginger and garlic, chopped chilli, and curry leaves. Cook for 1 minute, then add the chopped onions and saute until well browned (12 to 15 minutes). Add the salt and rice, toss gently, and cook for 2 to 3 minutes.

Remove from the heat. Add the yogurt and stir gently. Serve garnished with chopped coriander leaves, if desired.

Yield: Serves 4 with other dishes.

# Rice with Fenugreek

*Methi Pullao*

1 cup long-grain rice
1 1/2 cups water
1/2-inch piece fresh ginger
4 large cloves garlic
1 large onion
2 tablespoons vegetable oil
1/2 teaspoon cumin seeds
1 bay leaf
1/2-inch stick cinnamon
1 clove
1 cardamom pod
2 cups fresh fenugreek leaves
4 tablespoons fresh tomato puree
Salt, to taste
1/4 teaspoon ground turmeric

Wash the rice under running water, then let it soak in the 1 1/2 cups water. Grate the ginger and garlic. Slice the onion into thin half rounds.

In a large heavy-bottomed saucepan over medium heat, warm the oil. Add the cumin, bay leaf, cinnamon, clove, and cardamom pod. When the spices puff up and darken (1 to 2 seconds), add the grated ginger and garlic. Cook for 1 minute, then add the sliced onion and saute until the onion is well browned (about 10 minutes).

Coarsely chop the fenugreek leaves, add them to the pan, and cook for 2 to 3 minutes. Add the tomato puree, salt, and turmeric. Mix well, then add the rice and its soaking water. Stir gently, cover, increase the heat to high, and bring to a boil. Then reduce the heat to very low and cook for 25 minutes without uncovering the pan.

Turn off the heat and let the pan stand covered on the burner for 5 to 7 minutes. Then uncover, fluff the rice gently with a fork, and serve.

Yield: Serves 4 with other dishes.

# Spinach Rice

*Palak Pullao*

1 package (5 oz) frozen spinach
1 cup basmati rice
1 cup water
1 large onion
2 tablespoons vegetable oil
1 bay leaf
1 teaspoon cumin seeds
1/2-inch stick cinnamon
2 cloves
2 cardamom pods
Salt, to taste

Cook the spinach according to package directions. Drain well and grind to a smooth puree. Wash the rice, then let it soak in the 1 cup water. Slice the onion into thin half rounds.

In a large heavy-bottomed saucepan over medium heat, warm the oil. Add the bay leaf, cumin, cinnamon, cloves, and cardamom pods. Cook until the spices puff up and darken (1 to 2 seconds). Add the onion and saute until lightly browned (about 8 minutes). Add the rice and its soaking water, spinach puree, and salt. Stir gently, cover, increase the heat to high, and bring to a boil. Then reduce the heat to very low and cook for 25 minutes without uncovering the pan.

Turn off the heat and let the rice stand covered on the burner for 5 to 7 minutes. Then uncover, fluff the rice gently with a fork, and serve.

Yield: Serves 4 with other dishes.

# Rice with Kidney Beans

## *Rajma Biryani*

This needs a cooling raita or salad. Crunchy pappadams would add a nice touch. You could garnish it with fried onions, fried nuts, or chopped hard-cooked eggs.

1 cup basmati rice
1 cup water
1 large onion
1/2-inch piece fresh ginger
2 cloves garlic
3 tablespoons vegetable oil
1 bay leaf
1/2 teaspoon whole cumin seeds
Salt, to taste
1/2 teaspoon ground turmeric
1/2 teaspoon ground coriander seeds
1/2 teaspoon *garam masala*
1/2 teaspoon ground roasted cumin seeds
1 large tomato, chopped coarsely
4 tablespoons plain yogurt, beaten with a spoon
1 1/2 cups cooked kidney beans, drained

Wash the rice under running water, then let it soak in the 1 cup water. Slice the onion into thin half rounds. Grate the ginger and garlic.

In a large heavy-bottomed saucepan over medium heat, warm the oil. Add the bay leaf and whole cumin seeds. When the spices puff up and darken (1 to 2 seconds), add the grated ginger and garlic. Cook for 1 minute, then add the sliced onion and saute until golden brown (12 to 15 minutes). Reduce the heat to medium-low and add the salt, turmeric, coriander seeds, *garam masala*, and ground roasted cumin seeds. Saute for 1 minute. Add the tomato and cook until it is soft (about 5 minutes). Add the yogurt and cook for 2 minutes, stirring constantly. Add the kidney beans and rice with its soaking water. Stir very gently, cover tightly, increase the heat to high, and bring to a boil. Then reduce the heat to low and cook for 25 minutes without uncovering the pan.

Turn off the heat and let the pan stand covered on the burner for 5 minutes. Then uncover, fluff the rice gently with a fork, and serve.

Yield: Serves 4 with other dishes.

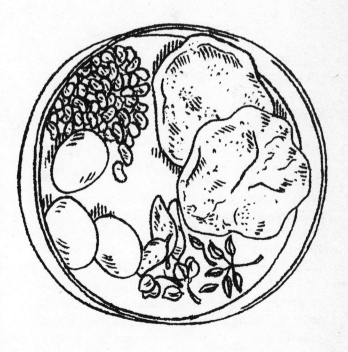

# Rice with Chicken

## *Murgh Biryani*

Garnishing a *biryani* in the traditional manner is quite an art. Fried onions, nuts, raisins, food coloring, edible silver foil, and rose petals are used imaginatively to please the eye and beguile the appetite.

1 1/2 pounds chicken breasts or thighs
1/2-inch piece fresh ginger
4 cloves garlic
2 medium onions
3 tablespoons vegetable oil
1/2 teaspoon whole cumin seeds
1/2 teaspoon ground coriander seeds
1/2 teaspoon ground cumin seeds
Salt, to taste
1/4 teaspoon cayenne pepper
1/2 teaspoon ground turmeric
6 tablespoons plain yogurt, beaten with a spoon
1 1/4 cups water
1 teaspoon *garam masala*
1 cup basmati rice
2 cloves
2 cardamom pods
1 bay leaf
1/2-inch stick cinnamon
1/4 cup *each* loosely packed fresh mint leaves
  and fresh coriander leaves, chopped finely
  (optional)

Skin and debone the chicken and cut it into 1-inch pieces. Grate the ginger and garlic. Chop the onions finely.

In a large heavy-bottomed skillet over medium heat, warm the oil. Add the whole cumin seeds. When they darken (1 to 2 seconds), add the grated ginger and garlic. Cook for 1 minute, then add the onions and saute until lightly browned (about 8 minutes). Add the ground coriander seeds, ground cumin seeds, cayenne, and turmeric. Cook for 1 minute. Then reduce the heat to medium-low, add the yogurt, and cook for 5 minutes, stirring constantly. Add the chicken pieces and 1/2 cup of the water. Cover, increase the heat to high, and bring to a boil. Then reduce the heat to low and cook for 20 minutes. Remove from the heat, add the *garam masala*, and set aside.

Wash the rice under running water, and put it in a heavy-bottomed pan along with the remaining 3/4 cup water, cloves, cardamom pods, bay leaf, and cinnamon. Cover, increase the heat to high, and bring to a boil. Then reduce the heat to low and cook until all the water is absorbed and the rice is tender (about 7 minutes).

Preheat the oven to 300°F. Spread half the rice mixture in the bottom of a clear ovenproof dish. With a slotted spoon pick out half the chicken from the sauce and layer it over the rice. Spread all the chopped mint and coriander leaves (if used) on top. Add a layer of the remaining rice and top with the remaining chicken. Dribble the sauce all over the rice and chicken, cover tightly with aluminum foil, and bake for 30 minutes. Remove from the oven and let stand for 5 to 7 minutes before serving.

Yield: Serves 4 with other dishes.

# Rice with Lamb and Coriander-Mint Chutney

## *Chutney Gosht Biryani*

This festive *biryani*, infused with the delicate fragrance of mint and coriander, has adorned banquets from the time of the Moghuls to this day.

**1 pound boned and defatted lamb or beef**
**1-inch piece fresh ginger**
**2 cloves garlic**
**2 medium onions**
**2 tablespoons vegetable oil**
**1/2 teaspoon whole cumin seeds**
**1/2 teaspoon ground coriander seeds**
**1/4 teaspoon ground cumin seeds**
**Salt, to taste**
**1/4 teaspoon cayenne pepper**
**5 tablespoons plain yogurt, beaten with a spoon**
**1/2 cup water**
**1/2 teaspoon *garam masala***
**1/2 cup coriander-mint chutney (optional)**

*Rice*

**1 cup basmati rice**
**3/4 cup water**
**2 cloves**
**2 cardamom pods**
**1/2-inch stick cinnamon**
**2 bay leaves**

Cut the lamb into 1-inch pieces. Grate the ginger and garlic. Slice the onions into thin half rounds.

In a large heavy-bottomed skillet over medium heat, warm the oil. Add the whole cumin seeds. When they darken (1 to 2 seconds), add the grated ginger and garlic. Cook for 1 minute, then add the sliced onions and saute until lightly browned (about 8 minutes). Reduce the heat to low and add the coriander seeds, ground cumin seeds, salt, cayenne,

and yogurt. Cook for 2 minutes, stirring constantly. Add the pieces of lamb and the 1/2 cup water. Stir, cover, and cook for 30 minutes. Remove from the heat, add the *garam masala*, and set aside.

Meanwhile, attend to the rice. Wash it under running water, then place it in a saucepan along with the 3/4 cup water, cloves, cardamom pods, cinnamon, and bay leaves. Cover and bring to a boil over high heat, then reduce the heat to very low and cook until all the water has been absorbed (about 7 minutes). The rice will be half cooked.

Preheat the oven to 300°F. Spread half the rice on the bottom of a clear ovenproof dish. Top it with all the chutney, then add a layer of the remaining rice. With a slotted spoon pick out the pieces of lamb from the sauce and layer them evenly over the rice. Dribble the sauce all over the lamb and rice, cover tightly with aluminum foil, and bake for 30 minutes. Remove from the oven and let stand for 5 to 7 minutes before serving.

Yield: Serves 4 with other dishes.

# Rice with Cottage Cheese and Mint

## *Podhina Paneer Biryani*

Versatile cottage cheese is used extensively in Indian cuisine to create dishes ranging from *koftas* (deep-fried dumplings), *biryanis* (spiced rice), and curries to combinations with a host of vegetables.

**1 recipe homemade cottage cheese**
**Vegetable oil, for deep-frying, plus 4 tablespoons**
  **vegetable oil**
**1/4 cup cashew nuts**
**1 cup basmati rice**
**1 cup water**
**2 medium onions**
**1/2-inch piece fresh ginger**
**2 cloves garlic**
**1 cup loosely packed fresh mint leaves**
**1/2 cup plain yogurt**
**1 1/2 cups fresh tomato puree**
**1/2 teaspoon cumin seeds**
**1 bay leaf**
**1/2-inch stick cinnamon**
**2 cloves**
**2 cardamom pods**
**Salt, to taste**
**1/2 teaspoon ground turmeric**
**1/4 teaspoon cayenne pepper**
**1/2 cup peas, fresh or frozen**

Dice the cottage cheese into 1/2-inch cubes. Warm the oil for deep-frying over medium heat and gently fry the cottage cheese cubes until golden brown on all sides. Drain on paper towels and set aside. Fry the cashews until golden brown. Drain on paper towels and set aside.

Wash the rice under running water, then let it soak in the 1 cup water. Slice the onions into thin half rounds.

In a large heavy-bottomed skillet over medium heat, warm the 4 tablespoons oil. Add the sliced onions and saute until browned (about 15 minutes). Remove half the onions with a slotted spoon and spread them out on a paper towel.

In the container of a food processor or blender, mince together the ginger, garlic, and mint. Transfer to a bowl. Beat the yogurt with a spoon and keep handy. Drain the rice, reserving 1/2 cup of the soaking water. Have the rice, minced ginger mixture, yogurt, and tomato puree close to the stove, since you will need to work fast now.

To the remaining onions and oil in the pan, add the cumin, bay leaf, cinnamon, cloves, and cardamom pods. Wait a few seconds, then add the ginger mixture. Reduce the heat to low and cook for 1 minute, then add the tomato puree and yogurt and cook for 5 minutes, occasionally stirring gently. Add the salt, turmeric, cayenne, peas, and fried cottage cheese cubes. Mix gently, then add the drained rice and soaking water. Cover tightly, increase the heat to high, and bring to a boil. Then reduce the heat to very low and cook for 30 minutes without uncovering the pan.

Turn off the heat and let the rice stand covered on the burner for 5 minutes. Then uncover, fluff the rice gently with a fork, and transfer it to a serving dish. Garnish with the reserved fried onions and cashews and serve hot.

Yield: Serves 4 with other dishes.

# Breads

In most North Indian homes, breads are prepared fresh for each meal. They are generally made from whole wheat flour and are cooked on a griddle or are deep-fried. They can be stuffed with lentils, potatoes, or other vegetables and served with a dry or wet vegetable, or a meat or poultry dish. *Chapatis* (pan-broiled wheat bread) and *parathas* (shallow-fried wheat bread) are eaten at most meals; the more elaborate *puris* (deep-fried wheat bread) and *kachodis* (stuffed wheat bread) are reserved for special occasions. *Naan*, a leavened bread, is traditionally cooked in a large clay oven known as a *tandoor*. Most villages in Punjab have a communal tandoor, where each evening women bring dough from their homes to be made into naan. The tandoor also serves as a meeting place where gossip is exchanged, recipes are passed on, and marriages are arranged.

# Pan-Broiled Wheat Bread
## *Chapati*

Most Indians eat with their fingers. *Chapatis* serve as a useful medium for transferring food from the plate to the mouth. A small portion of the bread is torn off, wrapped around a piece of meat or vegetable, and eaten. Leftover chapatis make delicious snacks when deep-fried, broken into 1-inch wedges, and sprinkled with salt and garlic powder. Chapati flour is available in all Indian grocery stores. It is finely sifted wheat flour, and breads made from it are softer in texture than breads made with regularly sifted flour.

**2 cups chapati flour *or* 1 cup whole wheat flour and 1 cup all-purpose flour**
**3/4 cup water**
**Ghee or butter**

Place the flour in a large mixing bowl and gradually add the water, mixing it in with your fingers. When all the water has been added, knead the dough until it is pliable (5 to 7 minutes). Cover with a damp cloth and let stand for 30 minutes.

Divide the dough into 8 equal parts and shape them into balls. Warm a griddle over medium heat. Roll one of the balls into a flat disk about 7 inches in diameter and about 1/16 inch thick, dusting with flour whenever necessary. Place it carefully on the griddle and let it cook for about 1 1/2 minutes. Flip it over. Let it cook for a minute, then press the surface gently with a folded cloth, and cook until both sides have brown specks and the disk puffs up in places (about 2 minutes). Transfer the disk to a large sheet of aluminum foil and rub 1/2 teaspoon butter or ghee on one side. Repeat with the remaining balls.

Alternatively, you can grip one edge of the disk with a pair of tongs and rest it on the grate above a medium-low gas burner. It will puff up immediately and gather light brown specks. Hold it for 1 to 2 seconds, toasting it all over, then flip it and toast the other side.

Stack the chapatis on top of each other as you cook them. They can be kept warm in a low oven. Serve warm.

Yield: Serves 4 with other dishes.

# Cottage Cheese-Wheat Bread
### *Paneer Ki Roti*

Apart from being nutritious, these chapatis are incredibly soft in texture.

**2 cups chapati flour *or* 1 cup whole wheat flour
   and 1 cup all-purpose flour**
**1/2 teaspoon salt**
**1 cup cottage cheese**
**1/2 cup water**
**Ghee or butter**

Place the flour in a large mixing bowl. Sprinkle the salt on top and mix it in with your fingers. Add the cottage cheese and work it into the flour. Gradually add the water and mix it in with your fingers until the dough is pliable, then knead the dough until it is smooth and elastic (5 to 7 minutes). Cover with a damp cloth and let stand for 30 minutes. Make chapatis following the directions on page 128. Serve warm.

Yield: Serves 4 with other dishes.

# Spinach-Wheat Bread
### *Palak Ki Roti*

**1 package (10 oz) frozen chopped spinach, thawed**
**1 medium onion**
**1/2-inch piece fresh ginger**
**Salt, to taste**
**2 cups chapati flour *or* 1 cup whole wheat flour
   and 1 cup all-purpose flour**
**5 tablespoons plain yogurt**
**Ghee or butter**

Squeeze out the excess water from the spinach. In the container of a blender or food processor, blend the onion, ginger, and spinach to a smooth paste. Transfer to a large mixing bowl. Add the salt and flour, and work the spinach mixture into the flour with your fingers. Add the yogurt and knead the dough until it is smooth and elastic (5 to 7 minutes). Cover with a damp cloth and let stand for 30 minutes. Make chapatis following the directions on page 128. Serve warm.

Yield: Serves 4 with other dishes.

# Deep-Fried Wheat Bread
## *Puri*

Puris are a treat that everyone should try at least once. They are easy to make and absolutely delicious. My young son, who is a fussy eater, can eat puris at anytime of the day, as can probably anyone who has eaten puris before. They go well with virtually everything that is on the menu. Although they can be made ahead of time and stacked in aluminum foil ready to be warmed in the oven, they are best when fried just before serving.

**2 cups chapati flour *or* 1 cup whole wheat flour
  and 1 cup all-purpose flour
2 tablespoons vegetable oil, plus vegetable oil for
  deep-frying
1 cup water, or as needed
1/2 teaspoon salt**

Place the flour in a large mixing bowl. Add the 2 tablespoons oil and the salt, and work them into the flour with your fingers. Gradually add the water and work it in with your fingers, then knead the dough until it is firm. Cover with a damp cloth and let stand for 15 minutes.

Divide the dough into 12 smooth, walnut-sized balls. Warm the oil for deep-frying over high heat. Dip an edge of one ball in a little oil from the pan and place it on a work surface. Roll it into a flat disk about 4 inches in diameter and slightly less than 1/4 inch thick, dusting it with a little flour for easier handling if necessary.

Gently slide the disk into the hot oil. To make it puff up, hold it under the oil and press it lightly with a slotted spoon when it bobs to the surface. After 1 minute flip it over and let it brown lightly on the other side. Remove with a slotted spoon and drain on paper towels. Make the remaining puris the same way. Serve warm.

Yield: Serves 4 with other dishes.

# Deep-Fried Onion-Wheat Bread
## *Pyaz Ki Puri*

This spicy dough can also be used to make Pan-Broiled Wheat Bread or Shallow-Fried Wheat Bread. Leftover dough may be stored in an airtight container in the refrigerator for several days.

**2 medium onions
1/2 teaspoon black peppercorns
1/2 teaspoon fennel seeds
1/4 teaspoon *kalonji* (onion seeds)
2 cups chapati flour *or* 1 cup whole wheat flour
  and 1 cup all-purpose flour
1/2 teaspoon salt
2 tablespoons vegetable oil
1/2 cup plus 2 tablespoons water**

Mince the onions. In the container of a coffee grinder, coarsely grind together the peppercorns, fennel seeds, and onion seeds. Place the flour in a large mixing bowl and add the minced onions, ground spices, salt, and the oil. Work them into the flour with your fingers. Gradually add the water and work it in with your fingers, then knead the dough until it is smooth and elastic. Cover with a damp cloth and let stand for about 15 minutes. Make puris following the directions on the left. Serve warm.

Yield: Serves 4 with other dishes.

# Egg-Filled Tortillas

## *Ande Parathe*

Flour tortillas provide a convenient alternative to the time-consuming Shallow-Fried Wheat Bread. Variations for their stuffing are endless—grated carrots or zucchini, sauteed mushrooms, diced cooked chicken, even some coriander-chutney mixed into the egg.

**1 medium onion**
**4 large eggs**
**2 tablespoons fresh tomato puree**
**Salt, to taste**
**1/4 teaspoon cayenne pepper**
**4 tablespoons vegetable oil**
**8 flour tortillas**

Chop the onion finely. In a large mixing bowl, break the eggs and beat them well. Add the tomato puree, chopped onion, salt, and cayenne and mix well.

Warm a griddle or skillet over medium heat and place a tortilla on it. Heat it for 1 minute, then flip it over. Spoon 3 tablespoons of the egg mixture on the tortilla and carefully fold it in half with a spatula. Don't worry if some of the egg seeps out. Spread 1/2 teaspoon of the oil on the top side. Let the tortilla cook for 2 to 3 minutes, then flip it over gently. Oil this side and cook for another 2 to 3 minutes. Slide the tortilla onto a plate, scraping onto the plate all the egg that may have seeped into the pan. Cook the remaining tortillas the same way, stacking them in a sheet of aluminum foil to keep warm. Serve warm.

Yield: Serves 4 with other dishes.

# Shallow-Fried Wheat Bread

## *Parathe*

Parathas are the shallow-fried version of chapatis and serve to make the meal a little more special. As children we always considered parathas a treat that made family dinners memorable.

**2 cups chapati flour *or* 1 cup whole wheat flour and 1 cup all-purpose flour**
**1/2 teaspoon salt**
**1 tablespoon vegetable oil, plus vegetable oil for shallow-frying**
**3/4 cup water**

Place the flour in a large mixing bowl and sprinkle the salt on top. Add the 1 tablespoon vegetable oil and mix it in with your fingers. Gradually add the water, mixing it in well with your fingers until you have a soft dough. Knead the dough until it is smooth and elastic (5 to 7 minutes). Cover with a damp cloth and let stand for 30 minutes.

Divide the dough into 8 equal parts and shape them into smooth balls with your hands. Flatten each ball lightly, dust with flour, and roll into a circle about 7 inches in diameter and 1/16 inch thick, dusting with more flour if necessary to prevent sticking.

Warm a griddle over medium-low heat. Place a paratha on it, cook for about 2 minutes, and flip it over. Spoon 1/2 to 3/4 teaspoon of oil onto the paratha and spread it evenly with the back of a spoon. Cook for 2 minutes, flip the paratha again, and spoon 1/2 to 3/4 teaspoon oil on this surface. Spread it with the spoon. Cook until brown spots appear on the surface (about 1 1/2 minutes). Remove the paratha and wrap it in aluminum foil to keep warm. Make the remaining parathas the same way. Serve warm.

Yield: Serves 4 with other dishes.

# Shallow-Fried
# Onion-Wheat Bread
## *Pyaz Ke Parathe*

Soaking peeled, halved onions in cold water for 5 minutes reduces their pungency, making it easier on the eyes when chopping them.

1 large onion
2 cups chapati flour *or* 1 cup whole wheat flour
   and 1 cup all-purpose flour
1/2 teaspoon salt
1 tablespoon vegetable oil
3/4 cup water

   Chop the onion very finely. Place the flour in a large mixing bowl. Add the salt, chopped onion, and oil and work them into the flour with your fingers. Gradually add the water, mixing it in with your fingers until you have a soft dough. Knead the dough until it is smooth and elastic (5 to 7 minutes). Cover with a damp cloth and let stand for 30 minutes. Make parathas following the directions on page 00. Serve warm.

Yield: Serves 4 with other dishes.

# Zucchini-Wheat Bread
## *Lauki Ke Parathe*

1 medium zucchini
1/2-inch piece fresh ginger
1 medium onion
Salt, to taste
2 cups chapati flour *or* 1 cup whole wheat flour
   and 1 cup all-purpose flour
2 tablespoons vegetable oil
1/2 cup water

Peel and grate the zucchini. Grate the ginger and onion. Place all the ingredients except the oil and water in a large bowl; add the oil and work it into the flour mixture with your fingers, adding the water to make a pliable dough. Knead the dough for a few minutes, then cover with a damp cloth and let stand for 30 minutes. Knead again and shape into parathas following the directions on page 131. Serve warm.

Yield: Serves 4 with other dishes.

# Fenugreek-Wheat Bread
## *Methi Ke Parathe*

If you can't find fresh fenugreek leaves, use half the amount of the dried herb in this recipe.

1 cup fresh fenugreek leaves
1/4 cup fresh coriander leaves (optional)
1 medium onion
Salt, to taste
1/4 teaspoon cayenne pepper
2 cups chapati flour *or* 1 cup whole wheat flour
   and 1 cup all-purpose flour
2 tablespoons vegetable oil
3/4 cup water

   Finely chop the fenugreek and coriander leaves. Chop the onion very finely. Place all the ingredients except the oil and water in a large mixing bowl. Add the oil and work it into the flour mixture with your fingers. Gradually add the water, kneading the dough until it is pliable. Shape into parathas following the directions on page 131. Serve warm.

Yield: Serves 4 with other dishes.

# Stuffed Wheat Bread

## *Kachodi*

Although somewhat laborious to make, kachodis should be tried at least once for their superb taste. The lentil stuffing, spiced with fennel seeds and coriander seeds, is special to Uttar Pradesh, where kachodis are often served at weddings and parties. Potatoes and Peas in Onion-Tomato Sauce and a raita make excellent accompaniments.

1 cup *dhuli urad dal* (black gram beans, split and hulled)
1/2-inch piece fresh ginger
4 cloves garlic
7 tablespoons vegetable oil, plus vegetable oil for deep-frying
1/2 teaspoon cumin seeds
Pinch crushed asafoetida (optional)
1/2 teaspoon cayenne pepper
Salt, to taste
2 teaspoons fennel seeds, coarsely ground
1 teaspoon ground coriander seeds
2 cups chapati flour *or* 1 cup whole wheat flour and 1 cup all-purpose flour, plus flour for rolling balls
2/3 cup water

Wash the beans and soak in plenty of water for 1 hour; drain. Transfer to the container of a blender or food processor along with the ginger and garlic. Blend to a smooth paste, adding a sprinkling of water if necessary.

In a large heavy-bottomed skillet over medium heat, warm 4 tablespoons of the oil. Add the cumin and asafoetida (if used). When the spices darken (1 to 2 seconds), add the bean paste, cayenne, salt, ground fennel seeds, and ground coriander seeds. Mix well and cook until the mixture is fairly dry (8 to 10 minutes). Transfer to a large bowl and set aside.

Place the flour in a large mixing bowl, and add salt and the remaining 3 tablespoons oil. Work them in with your fingers for a few minutes. Gradually add the water and knead until the dough is smooth and pliable.

Warm the oil for deep-frying. Divide the dough into 12 walnut-sized balls. Roll each ball in some flour and shape it into a disk about 2 inches in diameter and about 1/4 inch thick. Place 1 to 2 teaspoons filling in the center and gather up the edges to form a pouch. Pinch lightly to seal. Dip an edge in a little oil (or dust it with a little flour) and roll it into a disk about 4 inches in diameter and slightly less than 1/4 inch thick. Slide it gently into the oil. Wait a few seconds, then flip it over and press lightly with a slotted spoon to puff it up. Cook until lightly browned on both sides. Remove from the oil and drain on paper towels. Make the remaining kachodis the same way. Serve warm.

Yield: Serves 4 with other dishes.

# Pan-Broiled Leavened Bread
## *Naan*

Frozen *naan* are available at Indian grocery stores and can also be ordered by mail. Homemade *naan* can be frozen successfully, too. They should be warmed in the oven or on a griddle and buttered lightly before serving. Although they are traditionally baked in the oven, I find pan-broiling yields a softer, better *naan*.

1 cup whole milk
2 teaspoons sugar
2 tablespoons active dry yeast
4 cups all-purpose flour, plus flour for coating
  balls
1/2 teaspoon salt
1 teaspoon baking powder
2 tablespoons vegetable oil
2/3 cup plain yogurt
1 large egg, beaten lightly
Butter or ghee

Scald the milk, then let it come to room temperature. Add the sugar and yeast, stirring well to dissolve them. Let the mixture stand in a warm place until the milk is slightly frothy (about 15 minutes).

Place the flour in a large mixing bowl and add the salt, baking powder, oil, yogurt, and egg. Work them into the flour with your fingers. Gradually add the milk mixture and knead until you have a soft, smooth dough (5 to 7 minutes). Transfer the dough to a greased bowl, cover with a damp cloth, and let stand in a warm place until the dough has doubled in size (about 1 hour).

Punch down the dough and divide it into 12 equal-sized balls. Warm a griddle over medium heat. Roll one ball lightly in flour and with a rolling pin shape it into a circle 7 to 8 inches in diameter, dusting it with flour whenever necessary to prevent sticking. Place the *naan* on the griddle and cook until the surface bubbles lightly and the underside is lightly browned in spots (about 3 minutes). Flip it over and cook for another 3 minutes. Transfer to a dish and butter lightly. Cover with aluminum foil to keep warm. Make the remaining *naan* the same way. Serve warm.

Yield: Serves 4 with other dishes.

Chutney
&
Pickles

The homemade chutneys and pickles described here provide a wonderful glimpse into the world of Indian cuisine. Indian chutneys fall into two categories. Fresh chutneys are made daily in most homes and last about a week in the refrigerator. Made from ingredients such as fresh coriander, mint, curry leaves, onions, tomatoes, or tamarind, they are usually hot and sour to the taste. Preserved chutneys are bottled and can be kept for an indefinite period. Usually made from tomatoes, mangoes, apricots, and other fruits, they can be hot and spicy or sweet and sour. Recipes for both kinds of chutneys appear here. When making chutneys, use only the freshest ingredients.

Chutneys also make good marinades for meat and poultry. The food can then be barbecued or cooked in a pot. Chutneys add zest to *dals*, meat, poultry, seafood, or vegetable dishes; just add right before serving. Chutneys make good sandwich spreads; can be served as a dip for *pakoras*, *samosas*, and other snacks; and can be served at mealtimes to provide a contrast of flavors, add variety to the menu, and perk up flagging appetites.

Pickles are my favorite part of an Indian meal. Their different flavors—hot, sour, sweet, or spicy—add variety to the simplest of foods. Eating out in the homes of Indian friends and relatives is doubly pleasant because of the new kinds of pickles put out with the dinner. Each family has its own style of pickling, with subtle differences within the same family, making each jar of pickle unique. Not only are pickles eaten at mealtimes, they are also taken along on picnics, packed into lunch boxes, and tucked into food baskets for long journeys. When my family traveled by train from the South to the North in India—a two-day trip—my mother would carry along a complete dinner of *puris* (deep-fried wheat bread), *alu ki sabzi* (potatoes with cumin seeds and onions), and lots of pickled limes. Leftovers were usually consumed at breakfast.

In the preparation of pickles, as in all aspects of Indian cuisine, the influence of regional cooking and preserving techniques is felt keenly, so much so that different regions of the country have become famous for their pickles. In Punjab, a sweet-and-sour pickle of cauliflower, carrots, and turnips is eaten; in the South, limes are pickled with mustard seeds and fenugreek seeds; and the northern state of Uttar Pradesh is famous for its stuffed red chilli pickle and mango pickle. Indians believe that pickles serve to whet the appetite and help digest the food.

Pickles can be obtained ready-made in jars at Indian grocery stores and other specialty stores. Although these are tasty, they cannot compare in range, variety, and flavor to those made at home. Almost any fruit, vegetable, meat, fish, or poultry can be pickled—either in spices, oil, vinegar, or water. The pickle is then placed in the hot sun to tenderize and mature. Some pickles take a month or more to mature; others are ready within a week. The water-based pickles last about ten days in the refrigerator. Oil-based ones can last for years and actually taste better as time goes by. Unless otherwise specified, pickles don't need to be refrigerated. Since different vegetables and fruits are available only seasonally, pickles and preserves are the best way to eat them the year around.

When making pickles, use only the freshest produce and grind the spices at home if possible. Use clean, sterilized jars with nonmetallic lids and a wooden or stainless steel spoon for stirring. Set the pickles in the sun until they have become tender, shaking them often, then store them in a cool, dry place. Never use your hands to scoop out pickle, don't put back pickle that has been taken out of the jar, and don't let any water get into the pickle jar.

# Coriander-Mint Chutney
## *Dhania Podhina Chutney*

This fragrant fresh chutney can be found all over India. It is extremely nutritious and an excellent digestive aid. In many homes it is ground fresh every day and placed in the center of the table, ready to be eaten at any meal. It makes a delicious dip for crackers, vegetable sticks, and *pakoras*. Chutney sandwiches were our favorite school lunch when we were children, and *dals* tasted even better with heaping spoonfuls of chutney mixed in.

1 cup tightly packed fresh mint leaves
2 cups tightly packed fresh coriander leaves and tender upper stems
1 medium onion, quartered
1/2-inch piece fresh ginger
2 cloves garlic
1 green chilli (optional)
1/2 teaspoon cumin seeds
1/4 teaspoon *kala namak* (black salt)
Salt, to taste
2 tablespoons lemon juice

In the container of a blender or food processor, blend all the ingredients to a smooth paste. Transfer to a bowl and serve. Covered and refrigerated, this chutney will keep for a week.

Yield: Approximately 2 cups.

# Tomato Chutney
## *Tamatar Ki Chutney*

This chutney is cooked in the North Indian style, in which the tomatoes are simmered with whole spices.

1 pound ripe tomatoes
1/2-inch piece fresh ginger
4 cloves garlic
2 tablespoons vegetable oil
Pinch crushed asafoetida (optional)
1/2 teaspoon cumin seeds
1/2 teaspoon fennel seeds
1/4 teaspoon *kalonji* (onion seeds)
1/2 teaspoon peppercorns, coarsely crushed
2 cloves
2 cardamom pods
1/2-inch stick cinnamon
1 bay leaf
Salt, to taste
1/4 teaspoon cayenne pepper
1/2 teaspoon ground turmeric
1 tablespoon distilled white vinegar
1 teaspoon sugar

Chop the tomatoes coarsely. Mince the ginger and garlic. In a large saucepan warm them over medium heat. Add the asafoetida (if used), cumin, fennel, and onion seeds. Wait 1 to 2 seconds, then add the chopped tomatoes, black pepper, cloves, cardamom pods, cinnamon, bay leaf, salt, cayenne, and turmeric. Mix well, reduce the heat to low, cover, and cook for 30 minutes, stirring occasionally. Add the vinegar and sugar and cook for another 5 minutes. Remove from the heat and let cool. Transfer to a bowl and serve. In an airtight container in the refrigerator, this chutney should keep for a month.

Yield: Approximately 3/4 cup.

# Coconut Chutney
## *Thenga Chutney*

This popular chutney from South India traditionally accompanies all snacks. Because every housewife has her own recipe for it, there are innumerable versions to be found. The recipe given here is my favorite. As a variation, I sometimes mince 1 cup fresh mint leaves along with the coconut. This chutney makes a good dip for Dumplings with Spinach and Black-Eyed Peas.

1/2 fresh coconut cut into 1-inch pieces
1-inch piece fresh ginger
4 cloves garlic
1 green chilli (optional)
2 tablespoons water
Salt, to taste
4 tablespoons plain yogurt
1 small onion
1 tablespoon vegetable oil
1/2 teaspoon black mustard seeds
6 or 7 dried curry leaves

In the container of a blender or food processor, blend the coconut, ginger, garlic, chilli (if used), and the water to a smooth paste. Transfer to a large bowl and mix in the salt and yogurt. Slice the onion into thin half rounds.

In a small heavy-bottomed skillet over medium heat, warm the oil. Add the mustard seeds and curry leaves and cook until the seeds splutter. Add the sliced onion and saute until lightly browned (6 to 7 minutes). Add to the coconut mixture and stir well. Let cool, transfer to a bowl, and serve. Covered and refrigerated, this chutney will keep for a week.

Yield: Approximately 1 cup.

# Peanut Chutney
## *Moongphali Ki Chutney*

The recipe for this popular South Indian chutney was given to me by my friend Lynette. It makes an excellent dip for chips, vegetable sticks, and crackers. It goes well as part of the main meal, too. If you find it too thick, add some water until it has the consistency you like.

1 cup roasted, skinless, unsalted peanuts
4 tablespoons plain yogurt
Salt, to taste
1/4 teaspoon cayenne pepper
1 tablespoon vegetable oil
1 teaspoon black mustard seeds
Pinch crushed asafoetida (optional)
5 to 7 dried curry leaves
1 dried red chilli (optional)
Chopped fresh coriander leaves (optional)

In a spice grinder or food processor, grind the peanuts. Transfer to a small bowl and add the yogurt, salt, and cayenne. Mix well.

In a small skillet or butter warmer over medium heat, warm the oil. Add the mustard seeds, asafoetida (if used), curry leaves, and chilli (if used), and cook until the seeds splutter. Pour the spiced oil over the peanut mixture, mix well, let cool, and serve. You may also add some chopped fresh coriander leaves to the chutney before serving, if desired. Covered and refrigerated, this chutney will keep for a week.

Yield: Approximately 1 cup.

# Tomato Chutney with Coconut
### *Tamatar Nariyal Ki Chutney*

In this tomato chutney the flavors of coconut and onion seeds remain predominant and add a wonderful piquancy to the sweet-and-sour flavor. The recipe was given to me by my friend Rina Rao.

1 tablespoon vegetable oil
1 teaspoon fennel seeds
1/4 teaspoon *kalonji* (onion seeds)
1 1/2 pounds ripe tomatoes, chopped coarsely
Pinch salt
1/4 teaspoon cayenne pepper
1/2 cup unsweetened dried coconut flakes
2 tablespoons sugar
1/4 teaspoon ground ginger
2 tablespoons golden raisins
3 tablespoons distilled white vinegar

In a large heavy-bottomed skillet over medium heat, warm the oil. Add the fennel seeds and onion seeds. Wait 1 to 2 seconds, then add all the remaining ingredients except the vinegar. Cover, reduce the heat to low, and cook for 40 minutes, stirring occasionally. Remove from the heat and let cool slightly, then add the vinegar. Let cool completely, transfer to a bowl, and serve. In an airtight container in the refrigerator, this chutney will last for about a month.

Yield: Approximately 1 cup.

# Mango Chutney
### *Aam Ki Meethi Chutney*

Here is a simply cooked chutney with no mincing or frying involved; just add all the spices to the mango in a pan and let it simmer. The result—mouth watering!

1 pound green mangoes (about 1 large one)
1 teaspoon salt
2 tablespoons sugar
1/2 cup water
1/4 teaspoon cayenne pepper
1/4 teaspoon *kalonji* (onion seeds)
1/2 teaspoon *garam masala*
1/2 teaspoon peppercorns, coarsely crushed
1-inch stick cinnamon
2 cloves
2 cardamom pods
2 bay leaves
1 tablespoon golden raisins
1 clove garlic
1 tablespoon distilled white vinegar

Peel and cut the mango into 1-inch pieces. Scrape off as much flesh from the seed as possible, then discard the seed. Toss the mango pieces with the salt and let stand uncovered at room temperature for 2 hours. Then pat the pieces dry with a paper towel.

In a large saucepan over high heat, bring the sugar and the water to a boil. Reduce the heat to low and add all the ingredients except the vinegar. Cover and cook until the mango pieces are tender and the sauce thick (20 to 25 minutes). Remove from the heat and let cool, then mix in the vinegar. Transfer to a bowl and serve. In an airtight container in the refrigerator, this chutney should last for a month.

Yield: Approximately 3/4 cup.

# Tamarind-Mint Chutney

## *Imli Ki Saunth*

This chutney is traditionally served with *samosas* and *pakoras*. You can turn it into a side dish for dinner by adding sliced ripe bananas or chopped cooked potatoes. If its stay in the refrigerator has made it thick, you can dilute it with water to the desired consistency.

3/4 cup water
3 teaspoons tamarind paste
6 tablespoons sugar, or more if needed
1/2 teaspoon salt
1 1/2 teaspoons ground roasted cumin seeds
1/2 teaspoon *kala namak* (black salt)
3/4 cup mint leaves
1 green chilli
1/4-inch piece fresh ginger
1/4 cup fresh coriander leaves

Pour the water into a small heavy-bottomed pan over medium heat. Stir in the tamarind paste until it dissolves. Add the sugar, salt, cumin, and kala namak. Reduce the heat to medium-low and cook uncovered for about 7 minutes. Remove from the heat and let cool.

In the container of a blender or food processor, blend the mint, chilli, ginger, and coriander leaves to a smooth paste, adding a spoonful of water if necessary. Add to the tamarind mixture and stir well. Transfer to a bowl and serve. Covered and refrigerated, this chutney will keep about a week.

Yield: Approximately 1/2 cup.

# Pickled Limes

## *Nimbu Ka Achaar*

This pickle improves with age. My grandmother has pickles of different vintages, dating back from eight to sixteen years. She hands out small portions of it to privileged guests. A golden rule to keep pickle from spoiling is never to dip wet spoons in it or put back pickle that has been taken from the jar. For the best flavor, use homemade *garam masala*.

5 limes
1 1/2 teaspoons *garam masala*
1/2 teaspoon ground cumin seeds
1/2 teaspoon peppercorns, coarsely crushed
1/4 teaspoon crushed asafoetida
1/2 teaspoon cayenne pepper
4 teaspoons salt
4 tablespoons lime juice

Sterilize a 1-quart jar with a nonmetallic lid by boiling in water; dip the lid in the water for a few seconds also. Dry completely.

Wash and dry the limes thoroughly. Quarter the limes, keeping them attached at the base. In a small bowl combine all the spices and the salt. Rub the spice mixture into the limes, then place them base down in the jar. Pour the lime juice over the limes and fasten the lid tightly.

Keep this jar in the sun for the next 20 to 25 days, shaking it 2 or 3 times daily. Bring it in at night and keep in a warm place. The pickle will be ready to eat in a month; the flavor improves with age.

Yield: 5 pickled limes.

# Tomato Pickle with Garlic

## *Tomato Thokku*

Here is a recipe from the Andhra region in the South. If you are like me and love fenugreek, you will find yourself eating this pickle with just about everything from *puris* to pork chops! I often spread it on crackers, dot it with some cottage cheese, and perch an olive or some chopped cucumber on top for an attractive, wonderful-tasting hors d'oeuvre.

**2 pounds ripe tomatoes**
**10 dried curry leaves**
**Salt, to taste**
**1/4 teaspoon cayenne pepper**
**1/4 teaspoon ground turmeric**
**1/4 teaspoon fenugreek seeds**
**4 large cloves garlic**
**5 tablespoons vegetable oil**
**Pinch crushed asafoetida**
**1/2 teaspoon black mustard seeds**

Wash and dry the tomatoes completely. Chop coarsely, then place them in a large heavy-bottomed saucepan along with 5 of the curry leaves, salt, cayenne, and turmeric. Cover and cook over medium-low heat for about 1 1/2 hours, stirring frequently toward the end of the cooking time to prevent burning. You should be left with a very thick paste from the tomatoes. Uncover and let cool.

In a small heavy-bottomed skillet over low heat, dry-roast the fenugreek seeds until they turn a few shades darker (a few minutes). Grind and add to the tomato paste. Slice the garlic. Increase the heat to high under the skillet and warm the oil to the smoking point. Let it cool for a few seconds, then add the garlic slices. Cook for 1 minute, then add the asafoetida, the remaining 5 curry leaves, and mustard seeds. Cook until the seeds splutter, then pour the spiced oil over the tomato paste mixture. Stir well and let cool. Transfer to a bowl and serve. The flavor of this pickle improves with age.

Yield: Approximately 1/2 cup.

# Onions Pickled in Vinegar

## *Pyaz Ka Achar*

Pickled onions are usually served with a barbecued meal. Pick them out of the vinegar and arrange them in a small bowl. Once one batch of onions has been used up, more may be added to the same vinegar.

**1 pound small cooking onions or shallots**
**1 1/2 cups malt vinegar or distilled white vinegar**
**1/2 teaspoon sugar**
**Pinch salt**
**4 cloves**
**10 peppercorns**
**1 dried red chilli**

Leave the onions whole if they are small. Halve or quarter the large ones. Peel them and soak in salted water. Select a 1-quart jar with a nonmetallic lid. Wash and dry it thoroughly.

Place all the remaining ingredients in a medium pan and bring to a boil over high heat. Remove from the heat and let cool completely. Dry the onions well with a paper towel and place them in the jar. Pour the cooled vinegar mixture over them, ensuring that it covers the onions completely. Tighten the lid and let the jar stand in a cool, shady place for 4 to 5 days. Refrigerated in an airtight container, this pickle should last a month.

Yield: Approximately 2 cups.

# South Indian Lime Pickle
## *Limbehannu Uppinkai*

The distinctive spicing of the South gives this pickle a flavor very different from pickle made in northern India. The oil is added to protect the pickle from spoilage over the years. You can omit the oil if you think your pickle will be eaten soon. Serve it whenever you cook a South Indian meal.

5 green limes
4 tablespoons salt
1/2 teaspoon ground turmeric
Scant 1/2 teaspoon fenugreek seeds
1 tablespoon cayenne pepper
1/2 teaspoon crushed asafoetida
1/2 cup vegetable oil
1/2 teaspoon black mustard seeds

Wash and dry the limes thoroughly and cut them into 1-inch pieces. Sterilize a 1-quart jar with a nonmetallic lid by immersing it in boiling water for a few minutes. Dry completely with a paper towel. Place the limes in the jar, add the salt and turmeric, and shake to mix. Place the jar in the sun for 2 days, bringing it in at night and shaking frequently during the day.

In a small heavy-bottomed skillet over low heat, dry-roast the fenugreek seeds until they turn a few shades darker (a few minutes), then grind them and sprinkle on top of the pickle along with the cayenne and asafoetida. Do not mix the spices in. Increase the heat to high under the skillet and warm the oil to the smoking point. Remove from the heat and let cool slightly, then add the mustard seeds and cook until they splutter. Pour the spiced oil over the spices and limes in the jar; it will sizzle. Let the pickle cool, then cover and keep in the sun for a month, bringing it in at night and shaking the jar at least 3 or 4 times every day. The flavor of this pickle improves with age.

Yield: 5 pickled limes.

# Lime Pickle with Chillies and Ginger
## *Khatta Meetha Nimbu Ka Achar*

This is one of my mother's recipes—she excels in making sweet-and-sour pickles from limes, mangoes, and vegetables. Although not a big fan of sweet-and-sour pickles, I am completely hooked on this one. Whenever I make it, the limes are gone before they even have a chance to get completely tender in the sun.

4 green limes
10 green chillies (or equal or more amounts of milder peppers)
1-inch piece fresh ginger
2 tablespoons salt
1/4 teaspoon *kalonji* (onion seeds)
1/4 teaspoon fenugreek seeds
1/4 cup sugar
3 tablespoons distilled white vinegar

Sterilize a 1-quart jar with a nonmetallic lid by immersing it in boiling water for a few minutes. Dry completely with a paper towel. Wash and dry the limes, chillies, and ginger. Chop the limes into 1/2-inch pieces. Remove the stalks from the chillies and peel the ginger. Chop the chillies and ginger finely. Place the lime pieces and the chopped ginger and chillies in the jar and add the salt. Mix, cover tightly, and keep the jar in the sun for 10 days, shaking it occasionally.

Crush the onion seeds and fenugreek seeds coarsely. Add them to the jar along with the sugar and vinegar. Mix well, cover, and keep the jar in the sun for an additional month, bringing it in at night and shaking it frequently during the day.

Yield: 1 1/2 to 2 cups.

# Cauliflower and Carrot Pickle

## *Gobhi Gajar Ka Achar*

This is a pickle from the northern state of Uttar Pradesh, where I come from. We eat it often in our family because it is simple and quick to make and its sour taste appeals to us. The sourness comes from the mustard seeds and vinegar, which make the pickle increasingly sour as it matures in the sun.

**1 medium carrot (1/4 pound)**
**1/2-inch piece fresh ginger**
**2 cloves garlic**
**2 green chillies (optional)**
**3/4 pound cauliflower florets (1/2 inch to 3/4**
 **inch in diameter; about 3 1/2 cups)**
**1 tablespoon black mustard seeds**
**1/4 teaspoon fenugreek seeds**
**1 1/2 teaspoons salt**
**1/2 teaspoon ground turmeric**
**1/2 teaspoon cayenne pepper**
**1/2 teaspoon *kalonji* (onion seeds)**
**1/4 cup distilled white vinegar**

Select a 1-quart jar with a nonmetallic lid. Wash and dry it well. Wash and scrape the carrot and cut into 1/4-inch-thick rounds. Chop the ginger, garlic, and chillies coarsely.

Fill a large pan with enough water to cover the vegetables and bring to a rolling boil over high heat. Add the sliced carrot and cauliflower florets and blanch for 30 seconds. Drain immediately, spread on a paper towel, and let cool.

In the container of a clean coffee or spice grinder, grind together the mustard and fenugreek seeds. Place the cooled vegetables in the glass jar and add the chopped ginger, garlic, and chillies, the ground mustard and fenugreek, and the salt, turmeric, cayenne, onion seeds, and vinegar. Cover tightly and shake well to mix. Keep the jar in the sun for the next 5 to 7 days, bringing it in at night and shaking it often during the day. When the pickle has soured to your liking, refrigerate it. Covered and refrigerated, it should last for 10 days.

Yield: 3 1/2 to 4 cups.

# Turnip Pickle
## *Shalgam Ka Achar*

This recipe was given to me by my aunt, Swaroop Rani, who is the pickle expert of our family. Pickling is taken seriously in Indian homes. No matter what the season, some variety of fruit or vegetable is always pickled. The traditional method is sun curing, which tenderizes the pickle.

**1 1/2 pounds turnips (4 or 5 medium ones)**
**1 1/2 teaspoons black mustard seeds**
**1 teaspoon salt**
**1/2 teaspoon cayenne pepper**
**3 tablespoons vegetable oil**
**1/2 teaspoon fenugreek seeds**
**1/2 teaspoon ground turmeric**
**1 teaspoon whole fennel seeds**
**3 teaspoons ground fennel seeds**
**1 teaspoon *kalonji* (onion seeds)**
**3 tablespoons distilled white vinegar**

Wash and dry the turnips thoroughly. Halve each turnip and cut into 1/4-inch-thick slices. Pat them dry with a paper towel, then steam them over medium heat for 10 minutes, taking care that no water gets into the turnips. Let the turnips cool and pat dry again.

Sterilize a 1-quart jar with a nonmetallic lid by immersing it in boiling water for a few minutes. Dry completely with a paper towel.

In the container of a clean coffee or spice grinder, grind the mustard seeds finely. Transfer to a small bowl and mix in the salt, cayenne, and oil. Place the turnips in the jar and pour the spiced oil over them. Cover tightly, shake well, and place the jar in the sun for the next 4 to 5 days, bringing it in at night and shaking it 3 or 4 times daily.

In a small heavy-bottomed skillet over low heat, dry-roast the fenugreek seeds until they turn a few shades darker (a few minutes). Add to the jar along with the remaining ingredients. Cover and place in the sun for another 4 to 5 days, bringing it in at night and shaking it daily. The flavor of this pickle improves with age.

Yield: 2 to 3 cups.

# Barbecue Fare

*T*andoori, the style of cooking most frequently found in Indian restaurants, strangely enough has its roots outside of India. This concept of cooking food directly over live coals was introduced into the country by its Moghul conquerors, who brought it with them from the Middle East. Indians added their own distinctive spicing to it and a new cuisine was born.

Tandoori food gets its name from the tandoor, the clay oven in which the food is cooked. Imagine a huge vat with a small mouth, sunk into the ground, the bottom of which is lined with glowing coals, and you will have a good idea of what a tandoor looks like. Food on skewers is lowered through the opening and the heat is such that the food is cooked very fast. Infused with the aroma of clay and charcoal, the food acquires an indefinable but characteristic flavor.

Tandoori food can be prepared very easily at home. Using the basic techniques of marinating, you can achieve much the same result as a clay oven on a charcoal grill. Once you are familiar with this style of cooking, you will find that it offers a lot of scope for individual creativity. Any number of unusual ingredients can be combined to create new delicacies. The same principles can also be used to cook vegetarian fare.

This chapter contains a selection of traditional and not-so-traditional recipes all based on the tandoori style of cooking. All of the dishes can also be broiled in the oven. Vegetarians have not been forgotten and will find many simple and delicious dishes to acquaint them with the cuisine.

# Chicken in Tomato Puree

## *Tandoori Tamatar Murgh*

Tomato puree forms the base of the marinade for this dish. The flavor of grilled tomatoes and spices adds a delicious new dimension to the traditional tandoori flavor.

**2 pounds chicken drumsticks, thighs, or breasts**
**1/2-inch piece fresh ginger**
**4 large cloves garlic**
**Salt, to taste**
**1/4 teaspoon cayenne pepper**
**1 teaspoon ground coriander seeds**
**1/2 teaspoon ground cumin seeds**
**1 teaspoon *garam masala***
**1/4 teaspoon ground turmeric**
**1/2 cup canned crushed tomatoes in thick puree**

Skin the chicken, wash, and pat dry with a paper towel. Make deep cuts on the surface with a knife. Grate the ginger and garlic and combine in a small bowl with all the remaining ingredients. Mix well, then rub the paste into the chicken and let marinate for an hour at room temperature, or longer in the refrigerator.

Cook the chicken on a charcoal grill or in the broiler, basting with leftover marinade and turning to ensure even cooking. Serve hot.

Yield: Serves 4 with other dishes.

# Tandoori Chicken
## *Tandoori Murgh*

Among the best known and most popular dishes of Indian cuisine, tandoori chicken is the finest example of the tandoori style of cooking. Marinated in spiced yogurt and slowly grilled to perfection, it is a delight to eat. It is best served with Pan-Broiled Leavened Bread. However, if you are using boneless chicken breasts, you could also serve it stuffed into pita bread pockets, topped with a little raita or chopped tomatoes.

**2 pounds chicken drumsticks, breasts, or thighs**
**1/2-inch piece fresh ginger**
**4 cloves garlic**
**1/2 cup plain yogurt**
**Salt, to taste**
**1/4 teaspoon cayenne pepper**
**1 teaspoon paprika**
**1/2 teaspoon *garam masala***
**1/2 teaspoon ground coriander seeds**
**1/2 teaspoon ground cumin seeds**
**Dash lemon juice**

Skin the chicken, wash, and pat dry with a paper towel. Make deep cuts on the surface with a knife. Mince or grate the ginger and garlic. Transfer to a small bowl and add the yogurt and all the spices. Mix well, then rub the paste into the chicken and let marinate for an hour at room temperature, or longer in the refrigerator.

Cook the chicken on a charcoal grill or in the broiler, basting with leftover marinade and turning to ensure even cooking. Serve with a dash of lemon juice.

Yield: Serves 4 with other dishes.

# Tandoori Chicken in Tomato-Cream Sauce
## *Makhani Murgh*

Be sure to make some extra Tandoori Chicken when barbecuing. Creamy, buttery tomato sauce transforms it into this gourmet delight. This is an excellent party dish.

**1/2-inch piece fresh ginger**
**2 cloves garlic**
**1/2 cup butter**
**1 teaspoon ground coriander seeds**
**1 cup canned crushed tomatoes in thick puree**
**Salt, to taste**
**1/4 teaspoon cayenne pepper**
**1/4 cup whipping cream**
**1/2 teaspoon *garam masala***
**1 recipe Tandoori Chicken**

Grate the ginger and garlic. In a large heavy-bottomed skillet over low heat, melt the butter. Increase the heat to medium and add the grated ginger and garlic. Cook for a few seconds, then add the coriander. When it darkens (1 to 2 seconds), add the tomatoes, salt, and cayenne. Mix well and bring to a boil. Add the cream and *garam masala* and heat through. Add the cooked chicken and toss well with the sauce. Cook until the chicken is warm (5 to 7 minutes) and serve.

Yield: Serves 4 with other dishes.

# Tandoori Chicken in Tomato-Fennel Sauce

## *Rasedar Tandoori Murgh*

1/2-inch piece fresh ginger
2 cloves garlic
2 tablespoons vegetable oil
1 teaspoon fennel seeds
1/4 teaspoon *kalonji* (onion seeds)
1/2 teaspoon cumin seeds
1 cup canned crushed tomatoes in thick puree
1/4 cup water
Salt, to taste
1/4 teaspoon cayenne pepper
1 recipe Tandoori Chicken

Grate the ginger and garlic. In a large heavy-bottomed skillet over medium heat, warm the oil. Add the fennel seeds, onion seeds, and cumin seeds. When the spices darken (1 to 2 seconds), add the grated ginger and garlic. Cook for 1 minute, then add the tomatoes. Stir in the water, salt, and cayenne. Cover, reduce the heat to medium-low, and cook for 5 minutes. Add the cooked chicken, cover, reduce the heat to low, and cook for 15 minutes. Serve hot.

Yield: Serves 4 with other dishes.

# Chicken with Peanuts

## *Murghi Moonghphali*

2 pounds chicken drumsticks or thighs
1/2 cup roasted, skinless peanuts, ground
1-inch stick cinnamon
6 cloves
4 cardamom pods
1/2 teaspoon black peppercorns
1 teaspoon coriander seeds
1 teaspoon cumin seeds
1/2 teaspoon fenugreek seeds
1 dried red chilli (optional)
1 tablespoon white sesame seeds
1 teaspoon ground ginger
3 tablespoons unsweetened dried coconut flakes
8 to 10 dried curry leaves
Salt, to taste
1 tablespoon vegetable oil
6 tablespoons plain yogurt
Dash lemon juice

Skin the chicken pieces, wash, and pat dry with a paper towel. Make deep cuts on the surface with a knife. In a small heavy-bottomed pan over low heat, dry-roast the cinnamon, cloves, cardamom pods, peppercorns, coriander seeds, cumin seeds, fenugreek seeds, and chilli (if used). Cook until the spices puff up and darken (a few minutes), then add the sesame seeds, ginger, coconut, and curry leaves. Continue cooking until the sesame seeds and coconut turn brown (1 to 2 seconds). Let cool, then grind them finely.

In a small bowl combine the ground spices, ground peanuts, salt, oil, and yogurt. Rub this mixture well into the chicken pieces, cover, and let marinate at room temperature for 1 hour, or longer in the refrigerator. Cook the chicken on a charcoal grill or in the broiler until the chicken is golden and cooked through, turning to ensure even cooking. Serve with a sprinkle of lemon juice.

Yield: Serves 4 with other dishes.

# Chicken in Tomato Puree and Coriander-Mint Chutney

*Tandoori Chutney Murgh*

A delightful change from the usual barbecue fare, this dish can be assembled very quickly if you have some chutney in your refrigerator.

**2 pounds chicken drumsticks or thighs**
**1/4 cup coriander-mint chutney**
**4 tablespoons canned crushed tomatoes in thick puree**
**Salt, to taste**
**1 teaspoon *garam masala***
**Dash lemon juice**

Skin the chicken, wash, and pat dry with a paper towel. Make deep cuts on the surface with a knife. In a small bowl combine the chutney, tomatoes, salt, and *garam masala*, then rub over the chicken pieces and let marinate for 2 to 3 hours in the refrigerator.

Cook the chicken on a charcoal grill or in the broiler, basting occasionally with the leftover marinade and turning to ensure even cooking. Serve with a dash of lemon juice.

Yield: Serves 4 with other dishes.

# Chicken in Yogurt and Fenugreek

*Tandoori Methi Murgh*

I make this dish when I want to serve my guests something really different. Two of my favorite foods are featured here—grilled chicken and fenugreek. Accompany it with Potatoes in Creamy Yogurt Sauce and Pan-Broiled Leavened Bread.

**2 pounds chicken thighs**
**1 medium onion**
**3/4-inch piece fresh ginger**
**1 green chilli *or* 1/4 teaspoon cayenne pepper**
**Salt, to taste**
**6 tablespoons dried fenugreek leaves**
**6 tablespoons plain yogurt**
**1 teaspoon *garam masala***

Skin the chicken, wash, and pat dry with a paper towel. Make deep cuts on the surface with a knife. In the container of a blender or food processor, mince together the onion, ginger, and chilli. Transfer to a small bowl and add the salt, fenugreek, yogurt, and *garam masala*. Mix well, then rub into the chicken and let marinate overnight in the refrigerator.

Cook the chicken on a charcoal grill or in the broiler, basting with leftover marinade and turning to ensure even cooking. Serve hot.

Yield: Serves 4 with other dishes.

# Chicken with Tamarind
## *Murgh Khatai*

The tamarind in the marinade provides a pleasant tartness and a rich brown color to the chicken. This unusual, subtly flavored dish is well worth a try. It can be grilled a day in advance and served cold with crusty French bread, or warm with Green Bell Peppers with Vegetables and Cottage Cheese and Pan-Broiled Wheat Bread.

**2 pounds chicken thighs**
**2 teaspoons tamarind paste**
**2 tablespoons water**
**1/2 teaspoon sugar**
**Salt, to taste**
**1/4 teaspoon cayenne pepper**
**1 teaspoon ground ginger**
**1 1/2 teaspoons freshly ground black pepper**
**1 1/2 teaspoons ground coriander seeds**
**Vegetable oil, for basting chicken**

Skin the chicken, wash, and pat dry with a paper towel. Make deep cuts on the surface with a knife. Dissolve the tamarind in the water and add all the remaining ingredients except the oil. Rub this mixture over the chicken pieces and let marinate at room temperature for 1 hour, or longer in the refrigerator.

Cook the chicken on a charcoal grill or in the broiler, basting occasionally with a little oil and turning to ensure even cooking. Serve hot.

Yield: Serves 4 with other dishes.

# Chicken with Herbs
## *Murgh Tikka*

These chicken morsels, grilled with an herb marinade, are a delectable variation of tandoori chicken. The zesty flavor and aroma of the fresh herbs make this a popular dish. Serve it stuffed into pita bread pockets lined with lettuce and topped with chopped tomatoes.

**2 pounds skinned, boneless chicken**
**2 medium onions**
**3/4-inch piece fresh ginger**
**3 cloves garlic**
**1 large green bell pepper**
**1/4 cup fresh coriander leaves**
**1/2 cup fresh mint leaves**
**1/2 teaspoon ground coriander seeds**
**1/2 teaspoon ground cumin seeds**
**1 teaspoon *garam masala***
**Salt, to taste**
**1/4 teaspoon cayenne pepper**
**5 tablespoons plain yogurt**
**Dash lemon juice**

Wash the chicken and pat dry with a paper towel. Cut it into 1 1/2-inch pieces. Coarsely chop the onions, ginger, garlic, and bell pepper, and place in the container of a blender along with the fresh coriander and mint leaves. Mince well. Transfer to a large bowl and mix in the ground coriander, cumin, *garam masala*, salt, cayenne, and yogurt. Let the chicken marinate in this paste for 1 hour at room temperature, or longer in the refrigerator.

Thread the chicken onto skewers and cook on a charcoal grill or in the broiler, basting occasionally with all of the marinade and turning to ensure even cooking. Serve with a dash of lemon juice.

Yield: Serves 4 with other dishes.

# Chicken with Vinegar-Soaked Spices

*Murghi Raiwali*

The tart and spicy marinade for this chicken dish can be used for grilling fish too.

**1-inch stick cinnamon**
**8 cardamom pods**
**8 cloves**
**1 teaspoon black peppercorns**
**1 teaspoon coriander seeds**
**1 teaspoon cumin seeds**
**1 tablespoon black mustard seeds**
**1/4 cup distilled white vinegar**
**1-inch piece fresh ginger**
**4 cloves garlic**
**1 green chilli or 1/4 teaspoon cayenne pepper**
**Salt, to taste**
**2 pounds boneless chicken breasts**
**Vegetable oil, for basting**

Soak the cinnamon, cardamom pods, cloves, black peppercorns, coriander seeds, cumin seeds, and mustard seeds in the vinegar. Roughly chop up the ginger, garlic, and chilli (if using it) and add to the vinegar mixture. Let the spices soak for about an hour or longer. In the container of a blender, grind the mixture, including the vinegar, to a fine paste. Add the salt and cayenne (if using it).

Wash the chicken and pat dry with a paper towel. Make deep cuts on the surface with a knife. Rub the spice-vinegar paste over the chicken, cover, and let marinate for an hour at room temperature, or longer in the refrigerator.

Cook the chicken on a charcoal grill or in the broiler, basting occasionally with a little oil and turning to ensure even cooking. Serve hot.

Yield: Serves 4 with other dishes.

# Chicken with Chickpea Flour and Sour Cream

*Murgh Pakore*

Barbecued chicken *pakoras* taste even better than the deep-fried ones. They make delicious appetizers when served on a bed of onion rings marinated in vinegar.

**2 pounds chicken drumsticks, thighs, or breasts**
**6 tablespoons chickpea flour**
**6 tablespoons sour cream**
**1 1/2 teaspoons ground coriander seeds**
**1 teaspoon ground cumin seeds**
**Salt, to taste**
**1/4 teaspoon cayenne pepper**
**1 teaspoon *garam masala***
**1 teaspoon ground ginger**
**4 tablespoons water**
**1 cup bread crumbs**
**Vegetable oil, for basting**
**Dash lemon juice**

Skin the chicken, wash, and pat dry with a paper towel. Cut it into 2-inch pieces. In a small bowl combine the flour, sour cream, the spices, and the water to form a thick, smooth batter. Coat the chicken with it and let marinate for 1 hour at room temperature, or longer in the refrigerator.

Thread the chicken close together on skewers. Place the bread crumbs on a plate and roll the skewers in them, coating the chicken completely. Cook the chicken on a charcoal grill or in the broiler, basting frequently with the oil and turning to ensure even cooking. Sprinkle with lemon juice and serve.

Yield: Serves 4 with other dishes.

# Lamb Kebab with Yogurt

## *Boti Kabab*

1 pound boned and defatted lamb or beef
3/4-inch piece fresh ginger
4 cloves garlic
6 tablespoons plain yogurt
Salt, to taste
1/4 teaspoon cayenne pepper
1 teaspoon ground cumin seeds
1 teaspoon ground coriander seeds
1 teaspoon *garam masala*
Vegetable oil, for basting
Dash lemon juice

Cut the lamb into 1/2-inch pieces and pat dry with a paper towel. If the lamb seems tough, parboil the pieces until they are half done. Grate the ginger and garlic. In a large mixing bowl combine the yogurt, grated ginger and garlic, salt, cayenne, cumin, coriander, and *garam masala*. Mix well with a fork. Add the lamb pieces, toss to coat, and let marinate for 2 to 3 hours at room temperature, or overnight in the refrigerator.

Thread 5 or 6 pieces of lamb onto each skewer, leaving a little gap between the pieces. Spread any remaining marinade on top. Cook the kebabs on a charcoal grill or in the broiler, basting occasionally with a little oil and turning to ensure even cooking. Serve with a dash of lemon juice.

Yield: Serves 4 with other dishes.

# Ground Lamb Kebabs with Almonds

## *Badam Bhare Kabab*

1 medium onion
1/2-inch piece fresh ginger, grated
2 large cloves garlic, crushed
1/4 teaspoon ground turmeric
1 teaspoon *garam masala*
1 teaspoon ground fennel seeds
Salt, to taste
1/4 teaspoon cayenne pepper
2 raw eggs
1 pound lean ground lamb or beef

*Stuffing*

10 almonds
1 tablespoon white sesame seeds
2 hard-cooked eggs, peeled
3 tablespoons chopped mint leaves
2 tablespoons chopped fresh coriander leaves
Salt, to taste

Chop the onion finely. In a large bowl combine the chopped onion, grated ginger and garlic, turmeric, garam masala, fennel, salt, cayenne, and raw eggs. Add the ground lamb, combine thoroughly, and let marinate for an hour at room temperature, or longer in the refrigerator.

To make the stuffing, in a small heavy-bottomed pan over low heat, dry-roast the almonds until they smell roasted. Toast the sesame seeds until golden (1 to 2 seconds). Grind the nuts and seeds in a spice grinder. In a small bowl mash the hard-cooked eggs with a fork. Add the ground nuts and seeds, mint, coriander leaves, and salt and mix well.

Make 24 walnut-sized balls from the lamb mixture and flatten each one slightly. Place a flattened patty on your palm, drop a teaspoonful of the stuffing in the center, cover with another patty, and seal the edges. Flatten the patty lightly with your hands. Repeat with the other balls. Cook the kebabs on a charcoal grill or in the broiler, turning to ensure even cooking. Serve hot.

Yield: Serves 4 with other dishes.

# Grilled Ground Lamb
## *Seekh Kabab*

After tandoori chicken, *Seekh Kebabs* are probably the most popular item in tandoori cuisine. They are often served with Pan-Broiled Leavened Bread and Coriander-Mint Chutney. This dish is good served with Onion Rings and Onions Pickled in Vinegar on the side.

1 large onion
1/2-inch piece fresh ginger
4 large cloves garlic
Salt, to taste
1/4 teaspoon cayenne pepper
1/2 teaspoon ground coriander seeds
1/2 teaspoon ground cumin seeds
1 teaspoon *garam masala*
1 pound lean ground lamb or beef
Lemon juice

Coarsely chop the onion, ginger, and garlic. In the container of a blender or food processor, mince the chopped onion, ginger, and garlic with the salt, cayenne, coriander, cumin, and *garam masala*. Transfer the mixture to a large bowl, mix in the ground lamb, and let marinate at room temperature for an hour, or longer in the refrigerator.

Mold the lamb mixture onto skewers in 4-inch-long sausage shapes. Cook on a charcoal grill or in the broiler until browned on all sides, turning to ensure even cooking. To serve, slide them off the skewers, arrange on a platter, and sprinkle with lemon juice. Serve pickled onions or onion rings marinated in vinegar on the side.

Yield: Serves 4 with other dishes.

# Shrimp with Almonds, Yogurt, and Sesame Seeds
## *Badaami Til Jhinge*

These unusual shrimp kebabs make excellent hors d'oeuvres. Serve them on a bed of sliced tomatoes and Onion Rings. For an exotic touch add them to seafood soups and salads.

1 pound cleaned, shelled, deveined shrimp (about 24 shrimp)
1/2-inch piece fresh ginger
2 cloves garlic
15 almonds
6 tablespoons plain yogurt
Salt, to taste
1/4 teaspoon cayenne pepper (optional)
1 teaspoon freshly ground black pepper
2 tablespoons white sesame seeds
Dash lemon juice

Pat the shrimp dry with a paper towel. Grate the ginger and garlic. Grind the almonds in a coffee grinder. In a large bowl combine the yogurt, grated ginger and garlic, ground almonds, salt, cayenne, and black pepper. Mix well with a fork. Add the shrimp, toss well to coat, and let marinate at room temperature for an hour, or longer in the refrigerator.

Thread about 6 shrimp onto each skewer without leaving any gap in between. Spread all the remaining marinade on the shrimp. Lay all the skewers on a plate and sprinkle half the sesame seeds on top. With your fingers gently pat them into the marinade. Turn the skewers over and repeat with the remaining sesame seeds. Cook the shrimp on a charcoal grill or in the broiler until golden and tender. Serve with a dash of lemon juice.

Yield: Serves 4 with other dishes.

# Puree of Grilled Eggplant

## *Baingan Bharta*

This dish is a classic in Indian cuisine. I think it is the best way to cook an eggplant. Instead of grilling it, you may also bake it in the oven until tender. As a variation, a few spoonfuls of beaten yogurt can be added to the dish before serving. It is delicious stuffed into tomatoes and baked.

1 large eggplant (about 1 1/4 pounds)
1 medium onion
1/2-inch piece fresh ginger
2 cloves garlic
2 tablespoons vegetable oil
1/2 teaspoon cumin seeds
1/2-inch stick cinnamon
2 medium tomatoes, chopped coarsely
Salt, to taste
1/4 teaspoon cayenne pepper
2 tablespoons lemon juice

Lightly oil the surface of the eggplant. Grill it over a charcoal fire until lightly charred on the outside and cooked through. Allow to cool, then peel and discard the skin. Mash the eggplant well with a fork. Set aside.

Chop the onion finely. Grate the ginger and garlic. In a large heavy-bottomed skillet over medium heat, warm the oil. Add the cumin and cinnamon. When the spices darken (1 to 2 seconds), add the grated ginger and garlic. Cook for 1 minute, then add the chopped onion and saute until browned (about 10 minutes). Add the tomatoes and cook until soft (about 5 minutes). Add the salt and cayenne. Mix in the mashed eggplant, cover, reduce the heat to low, and cook for 5 to 6 minutes. Add the lemon juice, heat through, and serve.

Yield: Serves 4 with other dishes.

# Puree of Grilled Potatoes

## *Alu Ka Bharta*

The Indian version of mashed potatoes, this puree is lightly spiced and delicately roasted. You could serve it with an Indian or Western meal. After a barbecue, I often cook potatoes on low-burning charcoals, then save them for a later use. With a little heavier spicing, they are also good formed into croquettes and shallow-fried.

1 1/2 pounds potatoes
2 medium onions
Salt, to taste
1/4 teaspoon cayenne pepper
2 tablespoons butter
1 teaspoon cumin seeds
1/2 teaspoon ground coriander seeds
Lemon juice

Wash and dry the potatoes and wrap them individually in aluminum foil. Peel the onions and wrap each of them in foil, too. Place them directly on low-burning coals, turning them occasionally for even cooking.

Peel the cooked potatoes and mash them well with a fork. Remove any charred portions from the onions and slice thinly. Add them to the potatoes along with the salt and cayenne. In a large heavy-bottomed skillet over low heat, warm the butter. Increase the heat to medium and add the cumin seeds. When they splutter, add the coriander seeds. Immediately add the mashed potatoes and cook for 2 to 3 minutes. Mix in the lemon juice and serve.

Yield: Serves 4 with other dishes.

# Grilled Potatoes with Herbs
## *Alu Chaat*

This tasty, tangy treat can be served as a quick snack, a light meal, or as a salad accompaniment.

**1 1/2 pounds potatoes or sweet potatoes**
**1 green chilli *or* 1/4 teaspoon cayenne pepper**
**1/4 cup fresh coriander leaves and tender upper stems**
**Salt, to taste**
**1/2 teaspoon *kala namak* (black salt)**
**1 teaspoon ground roasted cumin seeds**
**1/4 teaspoon freshly ground black pepper**
**1/2 teaspoon ground ginger**
**Generous pinch *garam masala***
**3 tablespoons lemon juice**

Wash and dry the potatoes. Wrap them individually in aluminum foil and place them directly over low-burning coals or boil them in water until tender. When cooked, peel and dice them into 1/2-inch pieces and place them in a large bowl. Finely chop the chilli and fresh coriander. Add them to the potatoes along with the rest of the ingredients. Toss well to mix. Serve chilled or at room temperature.

Yield: Serves 4 with other dishes.

# Potatoes with Fennel and Yogurt
## *Saunf Ke Alu*

These potatoes are a good accompaniment to any barbecued meat dish.

**1 pound small potatoes (about 15 potatoes)**
**1/2 teaspoon salt, plus salt to taste**
**4 tablespoons plain yogurt**
**1 tablespoon ground fennel seeds**
**1/2 teaspoon ground cinnamon**
**3/4 teaspoon ground ginger**
**1/4 teaspoon cayenne pepper**
**1 tablespoon vegetable oil**

Wash the potatoes well. Leave the skin on if it is very thin or peel if desired. Place them in a large pan and fill with enough water to cover. Add the 1/2 teaspoon salt, cover, bring to a boil over high heat, and boil for 10 minutes. Drain and transfer to a large bowl. With a skewer or toothpick, prick the potatoes all over. Mix the remaining ingredients together and stir into the potatoes, toss well to coat, cover, and let marinate for an hour at room temperature, or longer in the refrigerator.

Thread 3 or 4 potatoes onto each skewer and cook on a charcoal grill or in the broiler until crisp and golden, basting occasionally with the marinade. Serve hot.

Yield: Serves 4 with other dishes.

# Mixed Vegetables with Yogurt

## *Tandoori Sabzi*

Vegetarians don't have to feel left out of barbecues. In this dish mixed vegetables marinated in the traditional tandoori style capture the flavor of this cuisine. Chunks of tofu marinated along with the vegetables can also be included. This dish can also be served in a sauce of your choice.

**8 baby potatoes, peeled**
**1 pound large cauliflower florets**
**2 medium green bell peppers**
**1 medium onion**
**4 tablespoons plain yogurt**
**4 tablespoons sour cream**
**3/4 teaspoon freshly ground black pepper**
**3/4 teaspoon ground coriander seeds**
**3/4 teaspoon ground cumin seeds**
**3/4 teaspoon *garam masala***
**1/2 teaspoon ground ginger**
**1/2 teaspoon garlic powder**
**Salt, to taste**
**1/4 teaspoon cayenne pepper**
**10 small mushrooms (about 1/4 pound)**
**8 cherry tomatoes**
**Dash lemon juice**

Put enough salted water to cover the potatoes and cauliflower in a pan, cover, and bring to a boil over high heat. Add the potatoes and cauliflower and cook covered for 8 minutes. Drain the vegetables immediately.

Cut the bell peppers and onion into bite-sized chunks. In a large bowl combine the yogurt, sour cream, and all the spices. Add all the vegetables, toss to coat, and let marinate at room temperature for an hour, or longer in the refrigerator.

Thread the vegetables onto skewers, making sure that each skewer has one of each vegetable.

Cook the skewers on a charcoal grill or in the broiler until browned and cooked through. Serve with a dash of lemon juice.

Yield: Serves 4 with other dishes.

# Desserts

*Mithai*, as desserts and sweetmeats are known in India, are much more than just the final course of a meal. They symbolize a sharing of the joyous moments in life with loved ones. The birth of a child in the family, the engagement of a son or daughter, a promotion, passing an important exam, and a religious festival are all events marked by distributing *mithai* among friends and relatives. At weddings, toward the end of the ceremony, the bride and groom feed each other a sweetmeat to "sweeten" their future together. *Mithai* also has a religious significance in India and is offered to the gods in temples to secure their blessings.

*Mithai* is sold everywhere, from wayside vendors with pushcarts to shops that specialize in sweets and savories. Such shops play an important role in the social lives of the people. Here you will see groups of earnest men discussing politics over *samosas* and cups of tea, giggling schoolgirls catching up with the latest gossip over a plate of *rasmalai*, or tired shoppers reviving themselves with *kulfi*. The glass cases displaying an enticing array of sweets and savories in different shapes, sizes, and colors beckon to the clientele to eat some more.

There are *mithais* to match every occasion and taste: *kheers*, made with milk and rice or vegetables; carrot, zucchini, or pumpkin *halwas*; *barfis*, created with thickened milk; and *kulfis*, which are a kind of Indian ice cream.

Generally, dessert is not served after an everyday Indian meal. It is reserved for special occasions. A plate of sliced or chopped up seasonal fruit or a bowl of dry-roasted fennel and cardamom seeds is customarily passed around.

Here are some fresh fruit serving suggestions: Mango with Cardamom, Cantaloupe with Lemon Juice and Mint, Watermelon with Ginger and Lemon Juice, Bananas in Sugar and Unsweetened Dessicated Coconut Powder, and Orange with *Kala Namak* (Black Salt).

# Rice Pudding with Cardamom
## *Chaval Ki Kheer*

Every year, on the religious full moon night of Sharad Purnima, my mother leaves a pot of *kheer* outside under the stars. The popular Hindu belief is that the gods will enrich it with nectar. Whether this is true or not, the *kheer* tastes fantastic the next day.

**1 cup long-grain rice**
**5 cups whole milk**
**5 to 6 tablespoons sugar**
**2 tablespoons golden raisins**
**2 tablespoons slivered blanched almonds**
**8 cardamom pods**
**3 to 4 drops rose essence (optional)**

Pick the rice over, wash well, and drain. In a large heavy-bottomed pot over high heat, bring the milk to a boil. Add the rice, reduce the heat to medium-low, cover, and cook until the rice is done and the pudding fairly thick (about 25 minutes), stirring occasionally. Add the sugar, raisins, and almonds and cook for about 4 minutes. Remove the seeds from the cardamom pods and grind the seeds. Remove the pudding from the heat and let cool, then add the ground cardamom and the essence. Serve chilled.

Yield: Serves 4.

# Almonds in Milk
## *Badam Basundi*

This dish is popular in the southern regions of India. Note that the almonds must be soaked overnight in water. A variation without the almonds tastes just as delicious.

**40 whole almonds**
**Few strands saffron (optional)**
**4 cups whole milk**
**5 tablespoons sugar**
**4 tablespoons golden raisins**
**6 cardamom pods**

Soak the almonds overnight in 1 cup water. Just before cooking, discard the water, then peel and grind the almonds to a fine paste. Warm 2 tablespoons of the milk and soak the saffron in it for 10 minutes. Pour the remaining milk in a large heavy-bottomed pan, add the sugar, and bring to a boil over high heat. Cook for 10 minutes, stirring constantly. Add the ground almonds, saffron milk, and raisins. Continue stirring over high heat for another 5 minutes. The mixture will have thickened somewhat by this time. Remove the pan from the heat and let cool at room temperature for 30 minutes. A thick layer of cream will have formed on top; stir it into the pudding.

Remove the seeds from the cardamom pods, grind them, and mix them into the pudding. Serve chilled in individual bowls.

Yield: Serves 4.

# Ricotta Cheese Dessert
## *Rasmalai*

A specialty of Bengal, *rasmalai* is traditionally made with steamed cottage cheese balls soaked in sweetened cream. It is a rich dish and quite irresistible. The recipe given here, although using unconventional ingredients, produces similar results with much less work. Note that this dish must be refrigerated for at least 2 hours before serving.

**8 cardamom pods**
**15 ounces whole milk ricotta cheese**
**1/2 cup sugar**
**1 pint half-and-half**
**Few strands saffron (optional)**
**6 almonds**
**6 cashew nuts**
**6 pistachio nuts**

Preheat the oven to 400°F. Remove the seeds from the cardamom pods and grind them coarsely. In a large bowl combine the ricotta, 1/4 cup of the sugar, and half the ground cardamom. Mix well with a fork, then spread it in a 3/4-inch-thick layer in an 8-inch by 8-inch baking dish. Bake until the top is lightly browned (about 35 minutes). Remove from the oven, let cool, and cut into squares.

Meanwhile, pour the half-and-half and the remaining 1/4 cup sugar in a large pan over high heat and bring to a boil, stirring occasionally. Reduce the heat to low, add the saffron, and simmer for 5 minutes. Chop all the nuts coarsely and add to the pan. Remove from the heat and carefully add the baked ricotta squares. Let the pudding cool at room temperature, then mix in the remaining ground cardamom. Refrigerate for at least 2 hours before serving.

Yield: Serves 4.

# Carrot and Milk Pudding
## *Gajar Ki Kheer*

I remember the first time my mother made this dessert. At the mere mention of carrots, I wrinkled up my nose and refused to have anything to do with it. When coaxed to try "just one spoonful," however, my views on carrot puddings underwent a radical change and I ate several helpings. This dessert certainly must be tasted to be believed.

1 tablespoon vegetable oil
2 cups tightly packed grated carrot (about 3/4 pound carrots)
2 cups whole milk
4 to 5 tablespoons sugar
1/4 cup whipping cream
2 to 3 tablespoons slivered blanched almonds and pistachios (optional)
6 cardamom pods
2 to 3 drops rose essence (optional)

In a large heavy-bottomed pan over medium heat, warm the oil. Add the grated carrot and saute for 5 minutes. Add the milk, increase the heat to high, and bring to a boil. Reduce the heat to low, cover, and cook for 5 minutes. Uncover the pan, increase the heat to medium, and stir in the sugar. Cook uncovered for 20 minutes. Remove from the heat and mix in the cream and nuts, then let the pudding cool to room temperature.

Remove the seeds from the cardamom pods, grind the seeds, and add them to the pudding along with the rose essence. Serve warm or chilled.

Yield: Serves 4.

# Mango Ice Cream
## *Aam Ki Kulfi*

This rich ice cream is often served at Indian weddings. It is frozen in small-sized clay cones, which are packed into terra-cotta vats filled with ice. Mango pulp is not always used in *kulfis*. For a quicker, lighter dessert, you can also mix some vanilla ice cream with the mango pulp using an electric hand blender. An absolute delight for mango lovers!

1 can (14 oz) sweetened condensed milk
1/2 pint plus 1/4 cup whipping cream
15 ounces canned mango pulp
2 to 3 drops *kewra* essence (optional)
5 cardamom pods
1 tablespoon slivered blanched almonds
1 tablespoon chopped blanched pistachio nuts

In a large bowl combine the milk and cream. Stir in the mango pulp and kewra essence. Remove the seeds from the cardamom pods, grind the seeds coarsely, and add to the mango mixture. Cover the bowl and freeze for about 8 hours. Garnish with the nuts just before serving.

Yield: Serves 4.

# Curdled Milk Dessert
## *Kalakand*

A restaurant near our house in Delhi was our favorite stop for Sunday lunches, which were inevitably topped off by some of their superb *kalakand*.

**1 1/2 cups whole milk**
**2 teaspoons plain yogurt, or more if needed**
**1 can (14 oz) sweetened condensed milk**
**4 cardamom pods**

Place the whole milk in a large heavy-bottomed pan and bring it to a boil over high heat. Stir in the yogurt and curdle the milk, adding a little more yogurt if necessary to curdle it completely. Add the condensed milk and cook uncovered for 20 minutes. Stir it occasionally, scraping it off the sides and bottom of the pan. Reduce the heat to low and cook uncovered until the milk mixture is a thick mass (about another 15 minutes), stirring occasionally to prevent burning. Remove from the heat and let cool to room temperature.

Remove the seeds from the cardamom pods, grind the seeds, and mix them into the dessert. Transfer to a greased baking dish and with a spatula spread it into a 1-inch-thick layer. Cover with plastic wrap and refrigerate for about 30 minutes, then cut into 1/2-inch diamond shapes or squares and serve.

Yield: Serves 4.

# Carrots in Milk and Nuts
## *Gajar Ka Halwa*

A popular dessert from Punjab, this is often served at weddings.

**1 pound carrots**
**1 1/2 cups whole milk**
**1/3 cup sugar**
**2 tablespoons golden raisins**
**1 tablespoon unsweetened desiccated coconut powder (optional)**
**2 tablespoons ghee or unsalted butter**
**6 cardamom pods**
**2 to 3 tablespoons slivered almonds**

Wash, dry, and grate the carrots. You should have about 4 1/2 cups. Select a wide-bottomed nonstick pan, pour in the milk, and bring to a boil over high heat. Add the grated carrots, mix well, cover, reduce the heat to low, and cook until most of the milk has been absorbed (about 15 minutes). Stir in the sugar, raisins, and coconut, increase the heat to medium, and cook uncovered until the liquid has evaporated (about 8 minutes). Add the ghee, increase the heat to high, and cook until a fairly dry consistency has been reached (about 10 minutes), stirring frequently.

Remove the seeds from the cardamom pods and grind the seeds. Remove the pan from the heat and mix in the ground cardamom. Transfer to a serving dish or individual bowls, garnish with slivered almonds, and serve.

Yield: Serves 4.

# Dumplings in Syrup
## *Gulab Jamun*

This popular dessert is recommended for people with a sweet tooth. The dumplings immersed in cardamom-flavored syrup become soft and delicious. I like to eat them warm, but they could also be served chilled. Note that the dumplings must soak in the syrup for at least 3 hours before serving.

**1 cup nonfat dry milk powder**
**1/2 cup all-purpose flour**
**1/2 cup whipping cream**
**1 tablespoon whole milk**
**1/4 teaspoon baking powder**
**Vegetable oil, for deep-frying**
**2 cups sugar**
**2 cups water**
**4 or 5 cardamom pods**

In a large bowl, place the milk powder, flour, cream, whole milk, and baking powder. Using your hands make a dough. Divide the dough into 20 equal portions and shape each into a smooth ball.

Warm the oil for deep-frying over medium-high heat. Reduce the heat to low, add as many balls as the pan can hold in a single layer, and cook until the balls are golden brown on all sides. Do not rush this process. Remove the dumplings and drain on paper towels.

In a large pan over high heat, combine the sugar and the water and bring to a boil. Stir once, reduce the heat to low, and simmer for 2 to 3 minutes. Remove from the heat. Transfer the fried dumplings to the syrup and let them cool completely.

Remove the seeds from the cardamom pods, grind the seeds, and add them to the syrup. Let the dumplings soak in the syrup for at least 3 hours before serving. Refrigerate unused portions.

Yield: Serves 4.

# Ricotta Cheese and Milk
## *Barfi*

Indian sweet shops offer a dazzling array of *barfis*, all made with different ingredients and offered in various shapes and colors and covered with thin edible silver sheets. The basic ingredient in many barfis is *khoya*, which is made by boiling down milk until it is thick and grainy. Since the process is too laborious to do at home, this recipe offers a convenient substitute.

**15 ounces whole milk ricotta cheese**
**15 ounces nonfat dry milk powder**
**5 tablespoons sugar**
**6 cardamom pods**

Place the ricotta, milk powder, and sugar in a heavy-bottomed pan over low heat. Let the cheese melt for 5 minutes, stirring it occasionally. Increase the heat to medium-low and cook uncovered for 20 to 25 minutes, stirring often. Scrape the bottom of the pan every time you stir and incorporate all the mixture sticking to the sides and bottom of the pan. Avoid letting it burn. By the end of the cooking time, the dessert should be very thick. Reduce the heat to low and stir for another 5 minutes. Remove from the heat.

Remove the seeds from the cardamom pods, grind the seeds, and mix into the dessert. Transfer the mixture from the pan to a greased 1-inch-deep casserole or pie dish, patting it into a 1/2-inch-thick layer. Let cool slightly, then cut into medium-sized squares or diamonds. Keep refrigerated until serving time.

Yield: Serves 4.

# Shopping Guide

## Connecticut

India Spice and Gift Shop
3295 Fairfield Ave.
Bridgeport, CN 06605
(203) 384-0666

## California

Bazaar of India
1810 University Ave.
Berkeley, CA 94703
(415) 548-4110

India Gifts and Foods
907 Post St.
San Francisco, CA 94109
(415) 771-5041

India Foods and Gifts
17820 S. Pioneer Blvd.
Artesia, CA 90701
(213) 865-3678

## Florida

Indian Grocery Store
2342 Douglas Rd.
Miami Beach, FL 33134
(305) 448-5869

## Illinois

India Gifts and Foods
1031 W. Belmont Ave.
Chicago, IL 60650
(312) 348-4392

## Maryland

India Emporium
68-48 New Hampshire Ave.
Tacoma Park, MD 20912
(301) 270-3322

## Missouri

Seema Enterprises
10616 Page Ave.
St. Louis, MO 63132
(314) 423-9990

## New Hampshire

East West Foods
Lamplighter Square
S. Nashua, NH 03062
(603) 888-7521

## New Jersey

India Bazaar
1665-180 Oaktree Rd.
Edison, NJ 08837
(201) 549-8444

## New York

Foods of India
121 Lexington Ave.
New York, NY 10016
(212) 683-4419

K. Kalistyan Orient Export Trading Co.
123 Lexington Ave.
New York, NY 10016
(212) 685-3451

Spice and Sweet Mahal
135 Lexington Ave.
New York, NY 10016
(212) 683-0900

Patel Discount Center
74-17 Woodside Ave.
Elmhurst, NY 11373
(718) 478-4547

India Trade Center
3359 Bailey Ave.
Buffalo, NY 14215
(716) 838-2149

## Pennsylvania

Bombay Emporium
294 Craft Ave.
Pittsburgh, PA 15213
(412) 682-4965

House of Spices
4605 N. 6th
N. Philadelphia, PA 19140
(215) 455-6870

## Texas

Apna Bazaar
5663 Hillcroft
Houston, TX 77036
(713) 785-6061

## Washington

Specialty Spice House
32040 23rd Ave. South
Federal Way, WA 98003
(206) 839-0922

## Wisconsin

India Groceries and Spices
4733 West North Ave.
Milwaukee, WI 53208
(414) 445-7003

## Canada

East India Company
2446 Cawthra Rd.
Mississauga, Ontario L5A 3K6

# INDEX

The Crossing Press
publishes a full line
of cookbooks.

Please call (toll-free)
800-777-1048
for a free catalog.